Please renew or return items by the date
shown on your receipt

www.hertsdirect.org/libraries

Renewals and   0300 123 4049
enquiries:

Textphone for hearing   0300 123 4041
or speech impaired

Hertfordshire

favourite
puddings

D0185231

Gregg's favourite puddings

Gregg Wallace

hamlyn

For Heidi, Tom and Libby.

An Hachette UK Company
www.hachette.co.uk

First published in Great Britain in 2010 by
Hamlyn, a division of Octopus Publishing
Group Ltd
Endeavour House
189 Shaftesbury Avenue
London
WC2H 8JY
www.octopusbooks.co.uk

First published in paperback in 2013

Copyright © Octopus Publishing Group Ltd 2010

Gregg Wallace asserts the moral right to be
identified as the author of this work

Some of the recipes in this book have previously
appeared in other books published by Hamlyn.

All rights reserved. No part of this work may be
reproduced or utilized in any form or by any
means, electronic or mechanical, including
photocopying, recording or by any information
storage and retrieval system, without the prior
written permission of the publisher.

ISBN: 978-0-600-62619-0

A CIP catalogue record for this book is available
from the British Library

Printed and bound in China

10 9 8 7 6 5 4 3 2 1

Both metric and imperial measurements are
given for the recipes. Use one set of measures
only, not a mixture of both.

Standard level spoon measures are used in
all recipes:
1 tablespoon = one 15 ml spoon
1 teaspoon = one 5 ml spoon

Ovens should be preheated to the specified
temperature. If using a fan-assisted oven, follow
the manufacturer's instructions for adjusting
the time and temperature.

Eggs should be medium unless otherwise
stated; choose free-range if possible and
preferably organic. The Department of Health
advises that eggs should not be consumed raw.
This book contains some dishes made with raw
or lightly cooked eggs. It is prudent for more
vulnerable people, such as pregnant and
nursing mothers, invalids, the elderly, babies
and young children, to avoid uncooked or lightly
cooked dishes made with eggs.

This book includes dishes made with nuts
and nut derivatives. It is advisable for those
with known allergic reactions to nuts and nut
derivatives and those who may be potentially
vulnerable to these allergies, such as pregnant
and nursing mothers, invalids, the elderly,
babies and children, to avoid dishes made
with nuts and nut oils. It is also prudent to
check the labels of preprepared ingredients
for the possible inclusion of nut derivatives.

contents

introduction

introduction

Anyone who watches *MasterChef* knows how much I enjoy puddings. People who stop and chat with me on the street tell me how much they enjoy the sight of me tucking into something sweet and sticky. Cab drivers yell out of their windows, 'Oi Gregg, make us a chocolate pudding!' In fact, my Twitter name is 'puddingface'.

I can't really explain why I love puddings so much. All children love the taste of something sweet and I never lost my sweet tooth. I still enjoy the same childlike delight when I get something heavenly.

It's not just sweetness, it's also texture, perhaps it's comfort. Definitely a good pudding is a luxurious thing. I suppose it could be seen as the height of decadence. Food is a necessity for life that's for sure. But a pudding, that is just pure indulgence. It is the last bit of the meal, usually your freshest memory from your lunch or dinner. It's the extravagant bit, the fun bit, the best bit! It is the ultimate comfort food, it's feel-good eating. Whether it's cold and soft like ice cream, or hot and filling like a pie. Deep and velvety like chocolate, or sharp and refreshing like lemon. The flavour and texture possibilities are endless. Pudding is a dish for every mood or occasion.

In learning to make puddings you are also mastering some serious culinary disciplines. Pastry, sugar work, decoration and presentation. Puddings also allow you to make the best use of the season's fruits. A fantastic pudding can simply be a ripe fruit served with cream or chocolate, or it can be as elaborate as fine pastry inside a sugar cage. There is no limit to your creativity, only your imagination.

It has taken a long time for Britain to be recognized by the rest of the world as having culinary talent. You can now eat in Britain as well as you can anywhere else in the world. It hasn't always been like this. For years, Britain's food was the laughing stock of Europe. Everybody sniggered and turned their noses up at our over-cooked meats and boiled vegetables. But even during these lean years there was one thing we excelled at, one area where Britain has been a market leader for centuries: our puddings.

This book is a collection of the greatest puddings ever made. Obviously I included all my favourites, but I also made sure that there was room for all the classics. My favourites may not be yours, but you are sure to find the recipes you love in here. I want everyone to know how to make a fantastic easy summer pudding. I think everybody should know how to crumble. If you can do that, you can then move on to a classic tarte tatin or a soufflé or a knickerbocker glory, or a black forest gâteau. Can you make or would you like to be able to make ice cream? When was the last time or have you ever attempted a proper Christmas pudding? It is all in here. Everything you need to know.

You can dip in and out of this book as you choose. Whenever the mood takes you, thumb through and decide which luxurious dessert you are going to attempt next. All good recipe books can be used this way, but this is also a very serious piece of work. It has all the instruction you will ever need to turn yourself into a very talented and knowledgeable pastry chef. Within this book, as well as all the fabulous recipes, you will find tips and information on all the dessert basics, such as how to make a sugar syrup, custard, brandy butter or a proper ganache. I'll take you through a number of sauces and the techniques you will need to make pastry and biscuits.

Whether you are an accomplished cook looking to add to your repertoire, or a pudding lover who desperately wants to know how to recreate restaurant dishes, or even a complete novice who would like to have a go, you will find what you are looking for in here. What I can guarantee is a lot of fun and many sumptuous flavours to lick off your fingers as you work.

Gregg

fruity
puddings

Blackcurrants and redcurrants in Cointreau

SERVES 4

finely grated rind and juice of 1 orange

2 tablespoons clear honey

3 tablespoons Cointreau

250 g (8 oz) fresh redcurrants

250 g (8 oz) fresh blackcurrants

whipped cream, to serve

Don't let the kids get to this, but for the grown-ups the slightly acidic currants mixed with orange-based booze is a winner.

1 Mix the orange rind and juice, honey and Cointreau together in a bowl.

2 Put the redcurrants and blackcurrants in a serving bowl, pour over the orange-flavoured syrup and chill overnight. Serve with whipped cream.

Exotic ruby fruit salad with cardamom

Cardamom is a heady delight. For me it conjures up visions of the Middle East, all deserts and big tents. You know what I mean. You can experiment here – this would work with many different fruits.

1 Prepare all the fruit according to its individual requirements. Cut into bite-sized pieces and put in a serving bowl.

2 Split open the cardamom pods, remove the little black seeds and grind them finely with a pestle in a mortar. Sprinkle over the fruit.

3 Combine the orange juice and liqueur in a jug, pour over the fruit and stir well to coat. Serve on its own or with vanilla ice cream.

SERVES 4–6

1.5 kg (3 lb) fresh tropical fruit, such as mango, papaya, pineapple, lychee, tamarillo, guava or physalis, or other fresh fruit of your choice

4 green cardamom pods

300 ml (½ pint) freshly squeezed ruby red orange juice

1 tablespoon Grand Marnier or Cointreau

Autumn pudding

SERVES 6–8

500 g (1 lb) cooking
apples, peeled, cored
and sliced

375 g (12 oz) fresh
blackberries

50 g (2 oz) soft light
brown sugar

2 tablespoons water

3 tablespoons port

8 slices of brown bread,
crusts removed

custard, to serve
(see page 170)

Exactly the same method as a summer pudding but this
time using autumn fruits. This is pure comfort food and
a perfect dish for your newly acquired custard skills.

1 Put the apples, blackberries, sugar and water in a heavy-based
saucepan. Cover and simmer gently for 10–15 minutes until soft
but not pulpy. Add the port and leave to cool. Strain the fruit through
a nylon sieve, reserving the juice.

2 Cut 3 rounds of bread to fit the base, middle and top of a 900 ml
(1½ pint) pudding basin. Shape the remaining bread to fit around
the side of the basin. Soak all the bread in the reserved fruit juice.

3 Line the base of the basin with the small round of bread, then
arrange the shaped bread around the side. Spoon in half the fruit
and place the middle-sized round of bread on top. Cover with the
remaining fruit, then top with the large bread round.

4 Cover with a saucer small enough to fit inside the basin and put
a 500 g (1 lb) weight on top. Chill overnight.

5 Turn out on to a serving plate, pour over any remaining fruit
juice and serve with warm custard.

Fruit compôte with summer garden fruits

A compôte is a great traditional preserving technique. It combines natural fruit flavours with a bit of added sweetness to match the fruits' tartness – all begging for the whipped cream.

1 Put the currants, blackberries and sugar into a heavy-based saucepan and cook gently, stirring occasionally, for 10 minutes until tender.

2 Remove from the heat and add the raspberries. Leave to cool. Serve with whipped cream.

Gregg's tip

You can make a compôte with just about any summer berry fruit. Simply adjust the amount of sugar to taste. It should keep well in the refrigerator for a few days, or can be frozen for up to three months.

SERVES 6

500 g (1 lb) mixed fresh redcurrants, blackcurrants and blackberries

125 g (4 oz) caster sugar

250 g (8 oz) fresh raspberries

whipped cream, to serve

Eve's pudding

Worth sinning for: light fluffy golden apple hidden under a sweet sponge topping. Lucky old Eve is all I can say.

1 Grease a 1.2 litre (2 pint) shallow ovenproof dish. Arrange the apples in the dish and sprinkle with the brown sugar.

2 Beat the butter and caster sugar together in a bowl until pale and fluffy. Add the eggs, one at a time, adding a little flour with the second egg. Fold in the remaining flour, then the hot water.

3 Spread the mixture evenly over the apples and bake in a preheated oven, 180°C (350°F), Gas Mark 4, for 40–45 minutes until golden brown. Serve with cream or custard.

SERVES 4

500 g (1 lb) cooking apples, peeled, cored and thinly sliced

50 g (2 oz) soft light brown sugar

125 g (4 oz) butter, plus extra for greasing

125 g (4 oz) caster sugar

2 eggs

125 g (4 oz) self-raising flour, sifted

1 tablespoon hot water

custard (see page 170) or cream, to serve

Apple snow

SERVES 4

500 g (1 lb) cooking apples, peeled and cored

65 g (2½ oz) caster sugar

2 tablespoons water

2 egg whites

finely grated rind and juice of ½ lemon

sponge fingers, to serve (see page 182)

Very light and creamy but still bags full of flavour. It looks so delicate and sophisticated – as if it's going to melt in moments just like snow.

1 Slice the apples into a saucepan, sprinkle with the sugar and add the water. Cover and cook gently for 10–15 minutes until the apples are tender.

2 Leave to cool slightly, then purée the apples in a blender or food processor or rub through a sieve. Leave to cool.

3 Whisk the egg whites in a grease-free bowl until stiff. Using a large metal spoon, fold the egg whites into the apple purée with the lemon rind and juice.

4 Spoon into glasses and serve with sponge fingers.

Nut and date baked apples

This is just a wonderful vision of autumn. Flaky almonds and sticky date nesting inside a baked apple. I can only describe it as apple with a toffee centre. Perfectly yummy.

1 Wash, dry and core the apples, then peel the top half. Place in an ovenproof dish with a lid.

2 Mix all the remaining ingredients together in a bowl and use to fill the centres of the apples.

3 Drizzle a little extra honey over the apples. Cover and bake in a preheated oven, 190°C (375°F), Gas Mark 5, for 30–40 minutes, basting the apples with the juices from time to time, until tender.

Gregg's tip

For almond and fig baked apples, mix 50 g (2 oz) melted butter, 250 g (8 oz) chopped dried figs, 3 tablespoons sherry and 6 tablespoons ground almonds together and use to fill the centres of the apples. Dot each apple with extra butter, cover and bake as above.

SERVES 4

4 cooking apples, such as Bramley

2 tablespoons chopped nuts, toasted

2 tablespoons chopped, stoned dates

juice of ½ lemon

2 tablespoons clear honey, plus extra for drizzling

½ teaspoon ground cinnamon

Apple pie with almond pastry

SERVES 4–6

ALMOND PASTRY

175 g (6 oz) plain flour,
plus extra for dusting

2 rounded tablespoons
ground almonds

125 g (4 oz) butter, at room
temperature, diced

25 g (1 oz) icing sugar,
sifted

1 egg yolk

2 tablespoons cold water

a little milk, for glazing

FILLING

750 g (1½ lb) apples,
peeled, cored and sliced,
or 500 g (1 lb) apples and
250 g (8 oz) fresh
blackberries

2 teaspoons freshly
squeezed lemon juice

125 g (4 oz) caster sugar

clotted cream, to serve

Let's face it, shouldn't everybody know how to make an apple pie? The almond pastry here is a nice touch. Ground almonds give a soft flavour and texture to a long-standing family favourite.

1 To make the pastry, mix the flour and ground almonds together in a bowl. Add the butter and rub in with your fingertips until the mixture resembles fine breadcrumbs. Stir in the icing sugar. Make a well in the centre. Mix the egg yolk and water together and add to the well. Mix to a rough dough with a fork.

2 Turn the dough out on a lightly floured surface and knead gently until quite smooth. Wrap in foil and chill in the refrigerator for 30 minutes before using.

3 If using blackberries, put them in an ovenproof dish and place in the oven while it is heating up to 200°C (400°F), Gas Mark 6.

4 Divide the pastry in half and roll out each half on a lightly floured surface to fit a 20 cm (8 inch) shallow pie plate. Line the plate with one piece of the pastry. Fill the pie with the fruit, the lemon juice, about 3–4 tablespoons blackberry juice from the warmed dish, if using blackberries, and the caster sugar. Moisten the edge and lay the other piece of pastry on top, pressing down the edge with your finger and thumb.

5 Make a small slit in the centre of the pastry top, prick lightly all over the top with a fork and brush with a little milk to glaze.

6 Bake in the centre of the preheated oven for 20 minutes. Reduce the oven temperature to 160°C (325°F), Gas Mark 3, and bake for a further 15–20 minutes. Serve warm with clotted cream.

Gooseberry and elderflower jelly

SERVES 6

500 g (1 lb) fresh gooseberries

450 ml (¾ pint) apple juice

4 elderflower heads

75 g (3 oz) caster sugar

1 teaspoon agar agar powder

75 ml (3 fl oz) single cream

6 fresh edible leaves or elderflower sprigs, to decorate

I love gooseberries – we grow both red and green varieties on the farm. I think you've got to be a bit clever here as all gooseberries taste slightly different depending on the season and when they were picked. You may have to add a little more or less sugar; let your taste buds decide.

1 Put the gooseberries in a saucepan with 300 ml (½ pint) of the apple juice and the elderflower heads, tied in a piece of muslin. Cover and cook gently until the gooseberries are soft. Remove the elderflower heads, squeezing out as much juice as possible.

2 Purée the gooseberries in a blender or food processor, then press through a nylon sieve to remove the tops and tails. Add the sugar and stir until dissolved, then set aside 75 ml (3 fl oz) of the purée.

3 Put the remaining apple juice in a small saucepan, sprinkle over the agar agar powder and leave to soak for 5 minutes. Bring to the boil, then reduce the heat and simmer for 3–4 minutes until the powder has dissolved. Add to the gooseberry purée. Turn the mixture into six 125 ml (4 fl oz) decorative moulds and chill until set.

4 To make the sauce, mix the cream with the reserved gooseberry purée. Turn the jellies out on to serving plates, surround each with some sauce and decorate with the leaves or elderflower sprigs.

Autumn fruit crumble

I am on record stating that I think any Englishman saying no to a fruit crumble should have his citizenship revoked. A delicious crunchy topping with steaming hot soft fruit beneath. Perfection.

1 Put the blackberries and apple slices in a bowl. Mix the cornflour and granulated sugar together and sprinkle over the fruit. Toss well until thoroughly coated. Turn the mixture into a 1.2 litre (2 pint) pie dish.

2 To make the crumble, sift the flour into a bowl. Add the butter and rub in with your fingertips until the mixture resembles coarse breadcrumbs. Stir in the demerara sugar, bran flakes and chopped nuts. Spoon the mixture over the fruit and flatten slightly with the back of a spoon.

3 Bake the crumble in a preheated oven, 190°C (375°F), Gas Mark 5, for 40–45 minutes until the fruit is tender and the topping light golden. Serve hot or cold with custard, cream or ice cream.

SERVES 4–5

250 g (8 oz) fresh blackberries

2 cooking apples, such as Bramley, peeled, cored and sliced

2 teaspoons cornflour

125–150 g (4–5 oz) granulated sugar, to taste

CRUMBLE

125 g (4 oz) plain flour

50 g (2 oz) butter, diced

50 g (2 oz) demerara sugar

25 g (1 oz) bran flakes, coarsely crushed

50 g (2 oz) chopped mixed nuts

custard (see page 170), ice cream (see page 148) or cream, to serve

Rhubarb crumble

SERVES 6

1 kg (2 lb) fresh rhubarb

125 g (4 oz) caster sugar

2 pieces of stem ginger, chopped

2 tablespoons stem ginger syrup

whipped cream or vanilla ice cream (see page 148), to serve

custard, to serve (see page 170)

CRUMBLE

250 g (8 oz) plain flour

125 g (4 oz) butter, diced

25 g (1 oz) caster sugar

25 g (1 oz) demerara sugar

You have found it. Congratulations. I am often asked for this recipe and here it is: my favourite pudding of all time. I just adore it. It's the crunchy, crumbly sweet topping with that absolutely incredibly sharp sweet rhubarb below. I would happily drown in a good rhubarb crumble.

1 Top and tail the rhubarb and remove the stringy skin. Cut the sticks into 2.5 cm (1 inch) lengths, put them in a large ovenproof dish and sprinkle with the caster sugar. Add the stem ginger and stem ginger syrup.

2 To make the crumble, sift the flour into a bowl. Add the butter and rub in with your fingertips until the mixture resembles fine breadcrumbs. Stir in the caster sugar.

3 Cover the rhubarb with the crumble and press it down lightly. Sprinkle the surface with the demerara sugar.

4 Bake in a preheated oven, 190°C (375°F), Gas Mark 5, for 40 minutes until golden brown. Serve hot with custard.

Gregg's tip

If you want to be a purist you can leave out the stem ginger and stem ginger syrup, but add an extra 25–50 g (1–2 oz) caster sugar.

Apricot and almond crumble

SERVES 4–6

500–750 g (1–1½ lb) fresh apricots

2 tablespoons granulated sugar (optional)

75 g (3 oz) blanched almonds (optional)

custard (see page 170) or lightly whipped cream, to serve

CRUMBLE

140 g (4½ oz) plain flour

60 g (2¼ oz) caster sugar

125 g (4 oz) ground almonds

175 g (6 oz) unsalted butter, plus extra for greasing

Apricots have such a wonderful perfume I'm surprised they aren't more popular. Almond and apricot is a marriage made in heaven.

1 Grease a 1.2 litre (2 pint) pie dish. Halve the apricots and remove the stones. If you wish, crack open a few of the stones and remove the kernels. Put the apricots and kernels, if using, in the bottom of the prepared pie dish. Sprinkle the granulated sugar and almonds over them, if using.

2 To make the crumble, mix the flour, caster sugar and ground almonds together in a bowl. Add the butter and rub in with your fingertips until the mixture resembles fine breadcrumbs. Spread lightly over the fruit.

3 Bake the crumble in a preheated oven, 200°C (400°F), Gas Mark 6, for 20 minutes. Reduce the oven temperature to 180°C (350°F), Gas Mark 4, and bake for a further 20–30 minutes or until golden brown. Serve hot with custard or lightly whipped cream.

Baked quinces

Baking quinces is a great way to sample them if you've never tried one before. They benefit greatly from some added sweetness, and the aromatic spices here complement their delicate flavour. A baked quince is a very good thing and very English indeed.

1 Peel and halve the quinces. Arrange them, cut-side up, in a roasting tin just large enough to hold them in a single layer.

2 Mix the honey and wine together, pour over the quinces and add the vanilla pod, cloves and star anise. Cover the tin with foil and bake in a preheated oven, 190°C (375°F), Gas Mark 5, for 30 minutes.

3 Remove the foil, baste the quinces and bake for a further 45–50 minutes, basting occasionally, until they are cooked and the juices become syrupy.

4 Meanwhile, mix all the ingredients for the lemon yogurt together in a bowl. Serve the quinces warm with the yogurt and pan juices.

SERVES 4

4 small quinces, about 250 g (8 oz) each

125 g (4 oz) clear honey

300 ml (½ pint) red dessert wine or full-bodied red wine

1 vanilla pod, split lengthways

4 cloves

2 star anise

LEMON YOGURT

125 ml (4 fl oz) Greek yogurt

1 tablespoon clear honey

1 teaspoon freshly squeezed lemon juice

Poires belle Hélène

Coor... this is right up there amongst my favourites. Steven Wallis won *MasterChef* in 2007 by making this beautiful dish in the final cook-off. Rich chocolate over juicy pear – you bet!

1 Peel the pears, leaving the stalks attached, and keep whole. Brush with the lemon juice.

2 Put the sugar in a large saucepan with the water. Heat gently, stirring, until the sugar has dissolved. Bring to the boil and boil for 2 minutes. Add the pears, lemon rind, cinnamon stick pieces and cloves. Cover, reduce the heat and simmer gently for about 20 minutes, turning once, until the pears are tender.

3 Drain the pears and put in a serving dish. Add the kirsch to the syrup and pour over the pears.

4 Make the chocolate sauce (see page 175). Once it has cooled slightly, transfer to a warm serving jug. Serve the pears with a generous covering of the chocolate sauce.

SERVES 6

12 small or 6 large ripe dessert pears

2 tablespoons freshly squeezed lemon juice

150 g (5 oz) caster sugar

600 ml (1 pint) cold water

2 strips of pared lemon rind

1 cinnamon stick, halved

6 cloves

4 tablespoons kirsch

Chocolate Sauce, to serve (see page 175)

Pears poached in rosé wine with cassis

SERVES 4

450 ml (¾ pint) Provençal rosé wine

50 ml (2 fl oz) crème de cassis

50 g (2 oz) caster sugar

2 strips each of pared lemon and orange rind

a squeeze of lemon juice

2 cinnamon sticks, bruised

4 cloves

4 large ripe dessert pears, peeled but left whole

vanilla ice cream (see page 148) or crème fraîche, to serve

I am very fond of a poached pear. I once watched Michel Roux cook one when I was working on *Saturday Kitchen*. The rosé just gives that little hint of acidity and the cassis a deeper hint of fruit.

1 Put the wine, cassis and sugar in a small, deep saucepan and bring slowly to the boil, stirring frequently, until the sugar has dissolved.

2 Add the lemon and orange rind, lemon juice and spices, return to the boil and carefully slip in the pears, submerging them as much as possible. Reduce the heat and simmer gently, turning the pears frequently so that they colour evenly, for 20 minutes or until tender.

3 Remove the pears with a slotted spoon and put them in a bowl. Bring the poaching liquid to the boil and boil until reduced by half and syrupy. Pour over the pears and leave to cool. Serve with crème fraîche or vanilla ice cream.

Cherry clafoutis

This grand old dame of puddings is an absolute French classic. Slightly sour cherries peeping through a light sweet batter. It's pudding perfection. Traditionally the pits are left in the cherries, but why anyone would want to do that is beyond me.

1 Pit the cherries over a bowl to reserve the juice.

2 Beat all the ingredients for the batter together in a large bowl.

3 Grease a 1.5–1.8 litre (2½–3 pint) pie or soufflé dish with the butter. Heat for a few minutes in a preheated oven, 200°C (400°F), Gas Mark 6, then add the cherries and any juice. Pour over the batter to cover.

4 Bake the pudding for 30 minutes or until well risen. Dust icing sugar lightly over the top and serve immediately.

Gregg's tip

You can substitute other stone fruit for the cherries if you want to break with tradition. Try ripe nectarines cut into segments or quartered plums.

SERVES 4

500 g (1 lb) ripe black cherries

15 g (½ oz) butter

sifted icing sugar, for dusting

BATTER

75 g (3 oz) plain flour

25 g (1 oz) caster sugar

3 large eggs

225 ml (7½ fl oz) milk

a few drops of vanilla extract

Poached figs with yogurt and honey

SERVES 4

300 ml (½ pint) red wine

50 g (2 oz) sugar

150 ml (¼ pint) crème de cassis

2 cinnamon sticks

2 strips each of pared lemon and orange rind

300 ml (½ pint) water

12 large firm ripe figs

SAUCE

150 g (5 oz) Greek yogurt

2 tablespoons clear Greek honey

1 teaspoon ground cinnamon

Nothing has quite got the texture of a fig – plummy and soft. It has an almost wine-like taste so poaching figs in wine brings out their flavour, and adding honey makes sure they retain their sweetness.

1 Put the wine, sugar, cassis, cinnamon sticks, lemon and orange rind and water in a saucepan and bring to the boil.

2 Add the figs to the pan, then cover, reduce the heat and simmer gently for 10 minutes until dark red and softened. Do not overcook, or the figs will fall apart.

3 Remove the figs with a slotted spoon and place in a serving dish. Bring the poaching liquid to a rolling boil, then reduce the heat and simmer until reduced by half and syrupy. Pour over the figs and leave to cool.

4 Meanwhile, mix all the ingredients for the sauce together in a bowl and set aside for the flavours to develop. Serve the figs at room temperature with a spoonful of sauce with each serving.

Baked bananas with chocolate fudge sauce

SERVES 4

4 firm bananas, skins
left on

1 tablespoon lemon juice

lightly whipped cream or
vanilla ice cream (see
page 148), to serve

SAUCE

100 ml (3½ fl oz) double
cream

125 g (4 oz) plain
chocolate, broken into
pieces

25 g (1 oz) unsalted butter

125 g (4 oz) golden syrup

**This just screams out fun, fun, fun! Soft sweet bananas
with just a bit of give. Smothered with chocolate fudge
sauce – come on, what else do you want?!**

1 Put the bananas in a shallow ovenproof dish. Brush the skins
with the lemon juice and bake in a preheated oven, 180°C (350°F),
Gas Mark 4, for 20 minutes or until the bananas have darkened in
colour and feel softened.

2 Meanwhile, put all the ingredients for the sauce in a small,
heavy-based saucepan and heat gently, stirring frequently, until the
chocolate has melted. Bring to the boil and boil for 2 minutes until
thickened slightly.

3 Transfer the bananas to warmed serving plates. Split lengthways
to reveal the flesh. Top with lightly whipped cream or vanilla ice
cream and serve with the hot sauce.

Strawberry cream meringue

Wow! This would make a fantastic centrepiece for any table. Be warned you will get messy but I can't think of anything nicer dropped down the front of my shirt.

1 Line 2 baking sheets with nonstick baking paper or lightly greased greaseproof paper.

2 Whisk the egg whites in a large, grease-free bowl until stiff peaks form. Fold in half the caster sugar and whisk again until very stiff and glossy. Lightly fold in the remaining sugar with a large metal spoon. Spread the mixture on the prepared baking sheets to form two 20 cm (8 inch) rounds.

3 Bake in a preheated oven, 110°C (225°F), Gas Mark ¼, for 4–5 hours or until completely dried out. Carefully lift the meringue rounds from the baking sheets and peel away the paper. Leave to cool on a wire rack.

4 For the filling, whip the cream and icing sugar together in a bowl until soft peaks form. Place one meringue round on a serving plate and spread with half the cream. Cover with half the sliced strawberries and top with the remaining meringue round. Spread the top with the remaining cream and cover with the remaining sliced strawberries.

5 Warm the jam in a small saucepan with the lemon juice until melted, then bring to the boil. Remove from the heat and leave to cool a little, but do not allow to set. Drizzle the melted jam over the strawberry topping, to give a sticky glaze. Serve within 1 hour of assembling.

SERVES 6

butter, for greasing (optional)

3 egg whites

175 g (6 oz) caster sugar

FILLING

300 ml (½ pint) whipping cream

1 tablespoon icing sugar

375 g (12 oz) fresh strawberries, hulled and sliced

3 tablespoons raspberry jam, warmed and sieved

2 teaspoons freshly squeezed lemon juice

Almond-stuffed peaches

4 large firm peaches, halved and stoned

75 g (3 oz) macaroons, crushed (see page 186)

50 g (2 oz) caster sugar

40 g (1½ oz) butter, softened, plus extra for greasing

1 egg yolk

½ teaspoon finely grated lemon rind

flaked almonds, to decorate (optional)

pouring cream, to serve

There's nothing quite like the nectar juice of a peach, it's somehow quite luxurious. The additional almonds are inspirational, mellow enough to not alter the beauty of the peach but giving it an extra dimension of texture.

1 Grease an ovenproof dish large enough to hold the peach halves in a single layer. Scoop a little flesh from the centre of each peach half and put in a bowl. Add the macaroon crumbs, sugar, 25 g (1 oz) of the butter, the egg yolk and lemon rind and beat until smooth.

2 Divide between the peach halves, shaping the stuffing into a mound. Top with flaked almonds, if you like, and dot with the remaining butter. Arrange in the prepared dish.

3 Bake the peach halves in a preheated oven, 180°C (350°F), Gas Mark 4, for 25–35 minutes until tender. Serve warm or cold with pouring cream.

tarts, flans and cheesecakes

New York cheesecake

BISCUIT BASE

175 g (6 oz) digestive biscuits, crushed

75 g (3 oz) butter, melted, plus extra for greasing

FILLING

1 kg (2 lb) full-fat soft cheese

275 g (9 oz) caster sugar

4 eggs, lightly beaten

40 g (1½ oz) plain flour, sifted

300 ml (½ pint) soured cream

finely grated rind of 1 lemon

fresh or drained canned strawberries, to decorate

This is rapidly becoming a pudding classic. Big and full of flavour – I just can't help myself. Every time I see one I think of tall buildings and hum Gershwin.

1 To make the biscuit base, grease a 23 cm (9 inch) loose-bottomed or springform cake tin. Process the biscuits in a food processor to fine crumbs. Melt the butter in a saucepan, add the biscuit crumbs and mix well. Press the crumb mixture evenly over the base of the prepared tin.

2 Place on a baking sheet and bake in a preheated oven, 180°C (350°F), Gas Mark 4, for 10 minutes. Leave to cool on the baking sheet while keeping the oven on.

3 To make the filling, beat the soft cheese and sugar together in a bowl, then mix in the eggs. In a separate bowl, beat the flour into the soured cream and lemon rind, then fold into the cheese mixture using a large metal spoon. Pour over the biscuit base in the tin. Bake in the oven for 45 minutes to an hour or until set. Leave for 3–4 hours until completely cool.

4 Run a round-bladed knife around the side of the cheesecake, then remove it from the tin. Transfer to a serving plate, decorate with the strawberries and serve.

Cinnamon cheesecake

SERVES 8

150 g (5 oz) plain flour,
plus extra for dusting

75 g (3 oz) butter, diced,
plus extra for greasing

40 g (1½ oz) caster sugar

500 g (1 lb) creamy soft
cheese

50 g (2 oz) soft light brown
sugar

25 g (1 oz) plain flour

150 ml (¼ pint) soured
cream

2 teaspoons ground
cinnamon, plus extra
to decorate

4 eggs

whipped cream,
to decorate

I just melt if I smell cinnamon. For me it's the closest a smell can get to a cuddle. I also adore cheesecakes: they are so big and hearty with just a hint of sourness in all that soft goodness.

1 Line and grease a 23 cm (9 inch) deep loose-bottomed flan tin. Sift the flour into a bowl. Add the butter and caster sugar and rub in with your fingertips until the mixture resembles fine breadcrumbs. Press into a stiff dough. Turn out on to a lightly floured surface and knead lightly until smooth.

2 Soften the creamy soft cheese in a bowl. Beat in the brown sugar and flour, then stir in the soured cream and cinnamon. Beat in the eggs, one at a time.

3 Put the dough in the prepared tin and press firmly with your knuckles to cover the base and side completely. Pour in the cheese mixture. Bake in a preheated oven, 160°C (325°F), Gas Mark 3, for 50 minutes–1 hour until set. Leave in the tin to cool completely.

4 Remove the cheesecake from the tin and transfer to a serving plate. Decorate with whipped cream and sprinkle cinnamon lightly over the top.

Baked cheesecake

Baked cheesecake is a little firmer and a little drier than an unbaked one. The sultanas in this are a clever addition, as they give a little extra moisture to the cheesecake, with a port-like punch flavour.

1 Line and grease a 20 cm (8 inch) loose-bottomed cake tin. Beat the butter, sugar and lemon rind together in a bowl until pale and fluffy. Beat in the cheese gradually, then mix in the egg yolks and beat thoroughly. Add the ground almonds, semolina, sultanas and lemon juice and mix well.

2 Whisk the egg whites with the cream of tartar in a separate, grease-free bowl until stiff. Using a large metal spoon, carefully fold the egg whites into the cheese mixture.

3 Spoon into the prepared tin and bake in a preheated oven, 180°C (350°F), Gas Mark 4, for 50 minutes–1 hour. Turn the heat off and leave the cheesecake in the oven to cool completely.

4 Remove the cheesecake from the tin, transfer to a serving plate and dust with icing sugar.

SERVES 6–8

75 g (3 oz) butter, plus extra for greasing

125 g (4 oz) caster sugar

finely grated rind and juice of 1 lemon

300 g (10 oz) curd cheese

2 eggs, separated

50 g (2 oz) ground almonds

25 g (1 oz) semolina

50 g (2 oz) sultanas

¼ teaspoon cream of tartar

icing sugar, for dusting

Blackberry and raspberry tart

SERVES 6

1 quantity Pâte Sucrée
(see page 177)

plain flour, for dusting

50 g (2 oz) ground
almonds

4–6 drops of almond
essence

1 quantity Rich Crème
Patissière (see page 172)

500 g (1 lb) blackberries
and raspberries

icing sugar, for dusting

A tart tart! Now there's a thing. This one makes very good use of soft fruit, both raspberry and blackberry having a fine tart quality. Serve as a dessert or with afternoon tea.

1 Roll the pastry out on a lightly floured surface and use to line a 20 cm (8 inch) flan tin or dish. Line the flan case with foil, fill with baking beans and bake in a preheated oven, 200°C (400°F), Gas Mark 6, for about 15 minutes until the pastry has begun to form a slight crust. Remove the foil and beans and bake for a further 10 minutes or until the pastry is dry and golden brown. Leave to cool in the tin on a wire rack, then carefully remove from the tin.

2 Stir the ground almonds and almond essence into the crème patissière and spread over the base of the flan case. Arrange the fruit on top. Dust with icing sugar before serving.

Linzer torten

SERVES 6

125 g (4 oz) butter

175 g (6 oz) icing sugar, sifted

1 egg, beaten

finely grated rind of 1 lemon

125 g (4 oz) ground almonds

125 g (4 oz) plain flour, sifted, plus extra for dusting

5 tablespoons raspberry conserve

2 tablespoons apricot jam, boiled and sieved

This is a fantastic tart. It's slightly fruity with just a hint of almonds, and beautifully moist. With a decent pot of tea I reckon I could possibly eat a couple of kilos of this.

1 Beat the butter and icing sugar together in a bowl until pale and fluffy. Beat in the egg and lemon rind, then fold in the ground almonds and flour and press together lightly into a dough. Wrap in foil and chill for 1 hour.

2 Carefully roll the dough out thinly on a lightly floured surface and use to line a 23 cm (9 inch) flan tin. Spread with the conserve, leaving a 2.5 cm (1 inch) border around the edge. Re-roll the trimmings and cut into shapes to form a lattice across the flan. Shape the remaining dough into a rope to fit around the edge and flatten with a fork.

3 Bake in a preheated oven, 190°C (375°F), Gas Mark 5, for 30 minutes. Leave to cool, then brush with the jam.

Strawberry crumble flan

This is really clever, very clever indeed. It's like an upside down crumble. In fact a kind of crumble, cheesecake flan. A sort of berryflancrumbcheese and it's every bit as delicious as it is clever.

1 To make the biscuit case, grease a 20 cm (8 inch) loose-bottomed flan tin. Process the biscuits in a food processor to fine crumbs. Melt the butter in a saucepan, add the biscuit crumbs and mix well.

2 Press the crumb mixture over the base and side of the prepared tin. Chill the biscuit case until firm.

3 To make the filling, beat the cream cheese, caster sugar, grated lemon rind and cream together in a bowl. Carefully transfer the chilled biscuit case from the flan tin to a serving plate. Fill the case with the cream cheese mixture, smoothing the top. Arrange the strawberries on top. Dust with icing sugar and serve cold.

SERVES 4–6

BISCUIT CASE

175 g (6 oz) ginger biscuits

75 g (3 oz) butter, plus extra for greasing

FILLING

250 g (8 oz) cream cheese, softened

75 g (3 oz) caster sugar

1 teaspoon finely grated lemon rind

4 tablespoons single cream

375 g (12 oz) small strawberries, hulled and halved if large

icing sugar, for dusting

Strawberry tartlets

Tartlet is a lovely word, isn't it? You don't have to feel guilty – you're not eating a whole tart. It's only a pretty little tartlet. Everybody knows how good strawberries taste, but glazed atop good pastry they reach a new dimension. I don't want to keep banging on about afternoon tea, but it could have been invented for these little blighters!

1 Roll the pastry out very thinly on a lightly floured surface and use to line 14 patty tins, then press a square of foil into each. Bake in a preheated oven, 190°C (375°F), Gas Mark 5, for 10 minutes or until golden. Leave to cool. Remove the foil, then carefully remove the tartlet cases from the tins.

2 Put the redcurrant jelly and water in a small saucepan and bring to the boil. Strain, return to the pan and reheat. Brush over the tartlet cases to glaze. Arrange the strawberries in the cases and brush with the remaining glaze. Leave to cool and set before serving.

MAKES 14

1 quantity Pâte Sucrée (see page 177)

plain flour, for dusting

4 tablespoons redcurrant jelly

1 tablespoon water

250 g (8 oz) strawberries, hulled and sliced

Rhubarb and lemon flan

SERVES 4–6

1 quantity Shortcrust
Pastry (see page 176)

FILLING

500 g (1 lb) rhubarb, cut
into 2.5 cm (1 inch)
lengths

1 egg

175 g (6 oz) caster sugar

25 g (1 oz) cornflour

finely grated rind of
1 lemon

10 tablespoons freshly
squeezed lemon juice

25 g (1 oz) butter

I adore rhubarb – there is no secret there. Balancing
sweetness with such a sour item as rhubarb is a skill.
Lemon juice gives it that tip of the tongue acidity which
highlights and emphasizes rhubarb's awesome flavour.

1 Roll the pastry out on a lightly floured surface and use to line a
25 cm (10 inch) flan tin.

2 To make the filling, arrange the rhubarb in circles in the flan case.
Put the egg, sugar, cornflour and lemon rind and juice in a saucepan,
beat together and slowly bring to the boil, stirring constantly, until
thickened. Add the butter and stir until melted. Spread the lemon
mixture over the rhubarb.

3 Bake the flan in a preheated oven, 180°C (350°F), Gas Mark 4,
for 30 minutes. Increase the oven temperature to 200°C (400°F),
Gas Mark 6, and bake for a further 15 minutes. Serve warm.

Gregg's tip

Use orange rind and juice instead of lemon. Reduce the amount
of sugar to 125 g (4 oz) and add ½ teaspoon ground ginger to the
filling ingredients.

Frangipane flan

Frangipane is made from almonds, like marzipan or Amaretto liqueur. They are flavours I would die for. Frangipane was actually invented by a perfumier who came up with the scent for the gloves of King Louis XIII of France. Pastry chefs got hold of it and hey presto! If you have never tried it I do urge you to give it a go.

1 Roll the pastry out on a lightly floured surface and use to line a 20 cm (8 inch) flan ring or tin. Line the flan case with foil, fill with baking beans and bake in a preheated oven, 200°C (400°F), Gas Mark 6, for 10 minutes. Reduce the oven temperature to 180°C (350°F), Gas Mark 4.

2 Remove the foil and beans from the flan case. Sprinkle the cake crumbs over the base of the flan case and arrange the cherries on top.

3 Beat the butter and caster sugar together in a bowl until pale and fluffy. Beat in the egg, flour, ground almonds and rosewater, if using. Spread the mixture over the cherries. Bake in the oven for 30–40 minutes until firm to the touch.

4 Dust with the icing sugar and serve the flan warm or cold.

SERVES 6

1 quantity Pâte Sucrée (see page 177)

plain flour, for dusting

50 g (2 oz) cake crumbs

425 g (14 oz) can pitted red cherries, drained

50 g (2 oz) butter

50 g (2 oz) caster sugar

1 egg

25 g (1 oz) plain flour

75 g (3 oz) ground almonds

1 teaspoon rosewater (optional)

1 tablespoon icing sugar, for dusting

Bakewell tart

SERVES 6

1 quantity Pâte Sucrée
(see page 177)

plain flour, for dusting

2 tablespoons raspberry
jam

4 eggs

100 g (3½ oz) caster or
granulated sugar

125 g (4 oz) unsalted
butter, melted and cooled

125 g (4 oz) ground
almonds

Oh my word, the controversy surrounding the Bakewell tart is incredible. There must be a hundred different claims for authenticity. Authentic or not this is a jolly delicious tart. It's the jam in it against that light sponge. I don't know why, it just feels naughty.

1 Roll the pastry out on a lightly floured surface and use to line a 20 cm (8 inch) fluted tart tin. Prick the base lightly with a fork and spread the jam over it.

2 Put a baking sheet in a preheated oven, 200°C (400°F), Gas Mark 6, to heat up. Beat the eggs and sugar together in a bowl until thick and creamy. Beat in the melted butter a little at a time, then fold in the ground almonds. Mix well, then pour the mixture into the prepared tart case.

3 Place the tin on the hot baking sheet and bake for 25–30 minutes or until set and golden brown. Serve the tart hot or cold.

Pecan pie

SERVES 8–10

1 quantity Pâte Sucrée
(see page 177)

plain flour, for dusting

FILLING

100 g (3½ oz) soft light
brown sugar

75 g (3 oz) treacle

75 g (3 oz) golden syrup

75 g (3 oz) butter, melted

1 teaspoon vanilla extract

finely grated rind of
1 lemon

4 eggs, beaten

175 g (6 oz) pecan nuts

A classic American pudding. Eating this will make you want to row across a river with George Washington. Those soft nuts set in amongst an almost toffee-like filling are simply stunning.

1 Roll the pastry out on a lightly floured surface and use to line a 28 x 18 cm (11 x 7 inch) baking sheet with sides. Chill for 30 minutes.

2 To make the filling, mix the brown sugar, treacle, syrup, melted butter and vanilla extract together in a bowl. Add the lemon rind and beaten eggs and mix well. Chop half the pecan nuts and add to the filling mixture. Pour into the prepared pastry case.

3 Arrange the remaining pecan nuts over the top of the pie. Bake in a preheated oven, 180°C (350°F), Gas Mark 4, for 45–50 minutes until the pastry case is golden brown and the filling has set. Leave to cool, then cut into squares to serve.

Gregg's tip

To make a chocolate pecan pie, add 2 tablespoons sifted cocoa powder to the filling mixture and sprinkle grated plain or milk chocolate over the baked pie.

Macadamia and vanilla tart

It's not a classic but my word this pudding has a light touch and big flavour. Milky, firm macadamias with the luxurious ever-popular big flavour of vanilla is a marriage made in heaven.

1 Sift the flour into a bowl. Add the butter and rub in with your fingertips until the mixture resembles fine breadcrumbs. Stir in the sugar. Add the egg yolk and enough of the water to mix to a firm dough, adding a little more if the dough feels dry. Turn the dough out on a lightly floured surface and knead until softened. Wrap in foil and chill for 30 minutes.

2 Roll the pastry out on a lightly floured surface and use to line a 23 cm (9 inch) loose-bottomed tart tin. Line the tart case with foil, fill with baking beans and bake in a preheated oven, 200°C (400°F), Gas Mark 6, for 15 minutes. Remove the foil and beans and bake for a further 5 minutes. Reduce the temperature to 160°C (325°F), Gas Mark 3.

3 Meanwhile, to make the filling, coarsely chop the macadamia nuts. Put the sugar, maple syrup and butter in a saucepan and heat gently until melted. Remove from the heat and beat in the vanilla paste and ground almonds, followed by the eggs. Stir in half the nuts.

4 Turn the filling mixture into the baked tart case and sprinkle with the remaining nuts. Bake the tart for about 25 minutes or until the filling forms a crust but remains quite soft underneath. Leave the tart to cool for 10 minutes, then serve with ice cream or cream.

SERVES 8–10

SWEET VANILLA PASTRY

175 g (6 oz) plain flour, plus extra for dusting

75 g (3 oz) lightly salted butter, diced

2 tablespoons Vanilla Sugar (see page 168)

1 egg yolk

2–3 teaspoons iced water

FILLING

200 g (7 oz) macadamia nuts

100 g (3½ oz) soft light brown sugar

250 g (8 oz) maple syrup

75 g (3 oz) unsalted butter

2 teaspoons vanilla paste

125 g (4 oz) ground almonds

4 eggs, beaten

ice cream or cream, to serve

Treacle tart

SERVES 4–6

1 quantity Shortcrust
Pastry (see page 176)

FILLING

250 g (8 oz) golden syrup

75 g (3 oz) fresh white
breadcrumbs

finely grated rind of
½ lemon

pouring cream, to serve

Oh yeah baby – you know it! Treacle tarts, so sweet they
bring on an itchy feeling deep in your throat. But they are
sticky and soft and everybody, I mean everybody, should
know what a good treacle tart tastes like.

1 Turn the dough out on to a lightly floured surface and knead
briefly. Roll the pastry out thinly to a 23 cm (9 inch) round and use
to line an 18 cm (7 inch) loose-bottomed flan tin. Chill the flan for
15 minutes.

2 To make the filling, mix the syrup, breadcrumbs and lemon rind
together in a bowl and spread over the flan case.

3 Bake the tart in a preheated oven, 200°C (400°F), Gas Mark 6, for
30 minutes. Serve warm with cream.

Gregg's tip

For a more traditional looking tart, chill the pastry trimmings along
with the case and use them to make a lattice pattern over the filling.

Banana and coconut tart

SERVES 6

butter, for greasing

200 g (7 oz) Shortcrust
Pastry (see page 176)

plain flour, for dusting

FILLING

7 tablespoons milk

75 g (3 oz) caster sugar

100 g (3½ oz) desiccated
coconut

2 eggs, beaten

1 tablespoon rum

5 bananas, sliced

juice of 1 lemon

whipped cream, to serve

SYRUP

1 tablespoon rum

4 tablespoons caster sugar

A fantastic slice of Caribbean flavours in a tart. Soft sweet banana and sweet sticky coconut – it tastes like sunshine. It couldn't be any more Caribbean if it played cricket.

1 Grease a 23 cm (9 inch) flan dish. Roll the pastry out on a lightly floured surface and use to line the prepared dish. Line the flan case with foil, fill with baking beans and bake in a preheated oven, 200°C (400°F), Gas Mark 6, for 10–15 minutes until the pastry has begun to form a slight crust. Remove the foil and beans and bake for a further 10 minutes or until the pastry is dry and golden brown.

2 To make the filling, put the milk in a small saucepan and bring to the boil, then leave to cool slightly. Mix the sugar and coconut together in a bowl, then stir in the beaten eggs. Add the milk, stirring, then return to the pan and cook gently, stirring constantly, until thickened. Add the rum and leave to cool. Toss the banana slices in the lemon juice, strain and reserve the juice.

3 To make the syrup, mix the rum, sugar and the reserved lemon juice together in a small saucepan. Heat gently until the sugar has dissolved, then boil to form a thick syrup. Pour the coconut mixture into the flan case. Arrange the banana slices over the top and pour over the syrup. Serve with whipped cream.

Cranberry tart

A fascinating tart – a real Christmas flavour but the cranberries lift it to a more refreshing level. Orange zest in the pastry means this tart makes your whole house smell delicious while it's in the oven too.

1 Sift the flour into a bowl. Add the butter and rub in with your fingertips until the mixture resembles fine breadcrumbs. Stir in the sugar and orange rind, then add the beaten egg and enough iced water to mix to a soft dough.

2 Turn the dough out on to a lightly floured surface and knead briefly. Roll out and use to line a 25 x 15 cm (10 x 6 inch) shallow rectangular tin. Trim the edges, reserving the trimmings.

3 Stir the cranberries into the mincemeat and spread the mixture over the base of the pastry case. Re-roll the pastry trimmings and use a cutter to cut into small stars or holly shapes. Arrange the shapes over the mincemeat mixture.

4 Brush the pastry with milk to glaze and sprinkle with a little caster sugar. Bake in a preheated oven, 190°C (375°F), Gas Mark 5, for 25–30 minutes until the pastry is golden brown. Sprinkle with caster sugar. Cut the tart into 8 squares and serve warm with whipped cream or warm pouring custard.

SERVES 8

250 g (8 oz) self-raising flour, plus extra for dusting

125 g (4 oz) butter, chilled and diced

75 g (3 oz) caster sugar, plus extra for sprinkling

finely grated rind of 1 orange

1 egg, beaten

250 g (8 oz) fresh or frozen cranberries, defrosted if frozen

250 g (8 oz) mincemeat

milk, for glazing

custard (see page 170) or whipped cream, to serve

Tarte tatin

SERVES 6

PASTRY

175 g (6 oz) plain flour, plus extra for dusting

75 g (3 oz) butter, chilled and diced

25 g (1 oz) caster sugar

1 egg yolk

2–3 tablespoons iced water

FILLING

50 g (2 oz) butter

50 g (2 oz) caster sugar

6 dessert apples, such as Cox's, peeled, cored and quartered

thick cream or crème fraîche, to serve

Classic brilliance and one of my all-time favourites. It's that combination of sweet juicy apple, buttery pastry and syrup that is just an incredible flavour and texture combination.

1 Sift the flour into a bowl. Add the butter and rub in with your fingertips until the mixture resembles fine breadcrumbs. Stir in the sugar. Add the egg yolk and enough of the water to mix to a firm, smooth dough. Wrap in foil and chill while you make the filling.

2 To make the filling, put the butter and sugar in a 20 cm (8 inch) ovenproof frying pan and heat on the hob until the sugar has melted and the mixture is golden. Add the apples and toss them in the syrup to coat. Cook for a few minutes until the apples begin to caramelize.

3 Roll the pastry out on a lightly floured surface to a round a little larger than the pan. Place it over the apples, folding over the edges of the pastry until it fits the pan neatly.

4 Bake in a preheated oven, 200°C (400°F), Gas Mark 6, for 35–40 minutes until the pastry is golden. Leave to cool in the pan for 5 minutes, place a large plate on top of the pan and invert the tart on to it. Serve warm with thick cream or crème fraîche.

Gregg's tip

Replace the apples with 5 peeled, cored and quartered pears and sprinkle the filling with 50 g (2 oz) walnut halves before covering with the pastry.

Plum and almond tart

1 quantity Pâte Sucrée
(see page 177)

plain flour, for dusting

1 tablespoon ground
almonds

500 g (1 lb) ripe dessert
plums, halved and stoned

50 g (2 oz) soft light brown
sugar

½ teaspoon ground
cinnamon

2 tablespoons flaked
almonds

cream, to serve

Not a hugely popular fruit these days, the plum. A shame because there are so many varieties, all with their own unique flavour. You could use whichever plums you wanted with this recipe and you will get a slightly different but always delicious result every time.

1 Roll the pastry out on a lightly floured surface and use to line a 20 cm (8 inch) flan tin. Line the tart case with foil, fill with baking beans and bake in a preheated oven, 200°C (400°F), Gas Mark 6, for 10 minutes.

2 Remove the foil and beans from the tart case. Sprinkle the ground almonds over the base of the tart case and arrange the plum halves on top, skin-side upwards, overlapping if necessary. Mix together the sugar, cinnamon and flaked almonds and sprinkle over the plums.

3 Bake the tart in the oven for 40 minutes. Serve hot or cold with cream.

Pear, hazelnut and cardamom flan

Cardamom is such a lovely flavour – fragrant and heady. This tart is such a pretty beast as well – slices of carefully arranged pear gives it a beautiful symmetry.

1 To make the pastry, sift the flour and salt into a bowl. Add the butter and rub in with your fingertips until the mixture resembles fine breadcrumbs. Stir in the sugar. Slowly add the egg and enough of the water to mix to a soft dough. Turn out on to a lightly floured surface and knead briefly. Wrap in foil and chill for 30 minutes.

2 Grease a 23 cm (9 inch) fluted flan tin. Roll the pastry out on a lightly floured surface and use to line the prepared tin. Prick the base all over with a fork and chill for a further 20 minutes.

3 Line the flan case with foil, fill with baking beans and bake in a preheated oven, 220°C (425°F), Gas Mark 7, for 10 minutes. Remove the foil and beans and bake for a further 10–12 minutes or until the pastry is dry and golden brown. Remove from the oven and reduce the oven temperature to 180°C (350°F), Gas Mark 4.

4 To make the filling, beat the butter and sugar together in a bowl until pale and fluffy, then beat in the eggs until incorporated. Lightly beat in all the remaining ingredients, except the pears. Pour the mixture into the baked flan case.

5 Peel and halve the pears, then scoop out the cores. Thinly slice each pear lengthways, being careful not to change the shape of the pears. Using a palette knife, carefully transfer the sliced pears to the flan case, arranging them neatly on the filling.

6 Bake the flan for 55–60 minutes until golden and firm in the middle. Serve the flan warm, sprinkled all over with a little caster sugar and with some cream.

SERVES 6

PASTRY

175 g (6 oz) plain flour, plus extra for dusting

¼ teaspoon salt

100 g (3½ oz) unsalted butter, diced, plus extra for greasing

2 tablespoons caster sugar

1 egg yolk

1–2 tablespoons iced water

FILLING

125 g (4 oz) unsalted butter, softened

75 g (3 oz) caster sugar, plus extra for sprinkling (optional)

2 small eggs, lightly beaten

75 g (3 oz) ground hazelnuts

25 g (1 oz) ground rice

seeds from 2 green cardamom pods, crushed

1 teaspoon finely grated lemon rind

4 tablespoons soured cream

3 small firm pears

cream, to serve

Tarte au citron

SERVES 6–8

PASTRY

250 g (8 oz) plain flour, plus extra for dusting

pinch of salt

125 g (4 oz) butter, diced

1 egg yolk

2–3 tablespoons iced water

FILLING

finely grated rind and juice of 3 large lemons

125 g (4 oz) caster sugar

2 eggs, plus 1 egg white

75 ml (3 fl oz) double cream

125 g (4 oz) ground almonds

pinch of ground cinnamon

TOPPING

2 lemons, thinly sliced

125 g (4 oz) caster sugar

cream or ice cream, to serve

This elegant and sophisticated dessert is a benchmark for professional pastry chefs. For me the standard was set by Michel Roux at The Waterside Inn. Time to match your skills against the best.

1 To make the pastry, sift the flour and salt into a bowl. Add the butter and rub in with your fingertips until the mixture resembles fine breadcrumbs. Add the egg yolk and enough of the water to mix to a soft, pliable dough. Wrap in foil and chill for 30 minutes.

2 To make the filling, put the lemon rind and juice and sugar in a bowl. Break in the eggs and add the egg white. Beat together well, then beat in the cream, ground almonds and cinnamon until thick and smooth.

3 Roll the pastry out on a lightly floured surface and use to line a 25 cm (10 inch) loose-bottomed flan tin. Prick the base all over with a fork and pour in the filling. Bake in a preheated oven, 190°C (375°F), Gas Mark 5, for 30 minutes or until the tart is set and golden. Leave to cool.

4 To make the topping, put the lemon slices with a little water in a saucepan and cook gently for 10 minutes or until tender. Remove and drain the lemon slices, reserving 75 ml (3 fl oz) of the liquid. Return the reserved liquid to the pan, add the sugar and cook, stirring, over a gentle heat until the sugar has dissolved. Bring to the boil, add the lemon slices and cook rapidly until they are well coated with thick syrup. Remove and use to decorate the tart. Leave to cool before serving with cream or ice cream.

Pumpkin pie

SERVES 6–8

PASTRY

300 g (10 oz) plain flour, plus extra for dusting

150 g (5 oz) unsalted butter, chilled and diced

3 tablespoons caster sugar

2–3 tablespoons iced water

FILLING

1 pumpkin, about 750 g (1½ lb), or 2 x 400 g (14 oz) can pumpkin purée

250 ml (8 fl oz) single cream

2 eggs

175 g (6 oz) maple syrup

4 tablespoons plain flour

1 teaspoon ground ginger

1 teaspoon ground cinnamon

lightly whipped and sweetened cream, to serve

This lovely pie makes clever use of a vegetable with another nod of the head to our cousins over the pond. It's a big boy's pud, this, and worth investing in a bigger spoon.

1 To make the pastry, put the flour into a food processor, add the butter and pulse until the mixture resembles fine breadcrumbs. Add the sugar and 1 tablespoon water and process briefly to a dough, adding the remaining water if the mixture is too crumbly. Alternatively, sift the flour into a bowl, add the butter and rub in with your fingertips until the mixture resembles fine breadcrumbs. Stir in the sugar and add enough of the water to mix to a soft dough. Wrap in foil and chill for 30 minutes.

2 If using fresh pumpkin, scoop out the seeds and fibres. Cut the pumpkin into large wedges and cook in a steamer over a saucepan of gently simmering water for 15–20 minutes until the flesh is tender. Scoop the flesh away from the skin with a spoon, put into a blender or food processor and blend until smooth. Transfer to a bowl. Alternatively, just put the canned pumpkin in a bowl. Add the cream, eggs, maple syrup, flour and spices and beat until evenly combined.

3 Roll the pastry out on a lightly floured surface and use to line a 23 cm (9 inch) loose-bottomed tart tin or a deep pie plate.

4 Pour the pumpkin mixture into the pastry case and place it on a baking sheet. Bake in a preheated oven, 200°C (400°F), Gas Mark 6, for about 30 minutes until the pastry is golden and the filling feels just firm to the touch. Serve warm with lightly whipped and sweetened cream.

Custard tarts

I've loved these for as long as I can remember. They evoke such fond memories of shopping with my grandparents in Rye Lane, Peckham. If I was good I would get a custard tart. Actually I'd get one even if I was naughty. My granddad was such a softy!

1 To make the pastry, sift the flour and salt into a bowl. Add the butter and fat and rub in with your fingertips until the mixture resembles breadcrumbs. Stir in the sugar. Beat the egg yolk with 2 tablespoons of the water and add to flour mixture to mix to a fairly firm dough, adding the remaining water as necessary.

2 Turn the dough out on to a lightly floured surface and knead briefly until smooth. Wrap in foil and chill for 30 minutes.

3 Grease 8 deep 5 cm (2 inch) sections of a muffin tin. Roll the pastry out thinly on a lightly floured surface. Cut out eight 7 cm (3 inch) rounds, using a large pastry cutter or small saucer as a guide, and use to line the prepared tins. Press a square of foil into each. Bake in a preheated oven, 200°C (400°F), Gas Mark 6, for 12–15 minutes until set but not brown. Remove the foil. Reduce the oven temperature to 160°C (325°F), Gas Mark 3.

4 To make the custard, warm the milk in a saucepan. Meanwhile, beat the eggs and sugar together in a bowl. Stir the warm milk into the egg mixture and add the vanilla extract. Strain the custard into the pastry cases.

5 Sprinkle the tops with nutmeg and bake the tarts in the centre of the oven for 15–20 minutes until the custard is set. Serve warm or cool.

MAKES 8

SWEET PASTRY

250 g (8 oz) plain flour, plus extra for dusting

pinch of salt

50 g (2 oz) butter, plus extra for greasing

50 g (2 oz) white vegetable fat

25 g (1 oz) caster sugar

1 egg yolk

2–3 tablespoons iced water

CUSTARD

450 ml (¾ pint) milk

2 eggs

2–3 teaspoons caster sugar

¼ teaspoon vanilla extract

freshly grated nutmeg, for sprinkling

Portuguese custard tarts

These are brilliant – I really love them. In Lisbon, you'll find these famous tarts piled high in café windows. This version uses delicious cinnamon pastry but for a more authentic touch use puff pastry instead.

1 Mix the vanilla sugar with the cinnamon. Cut the pastry in half and roll out each piece on a lightly floured surface to 20 cm (8 inches) square. Sprinkle one square with the spiced sugar and position the second square on top. Re-roll the pastry thinly to a 40 x 30 cm (16 x 12 inch) rectangle and cut out twelve 10 cm (4 inch) squares.

2 Use the pastry rounds to line the sections of a nonstick muffin tin, pressing them firmly into the base and around the side. Press a square of foil into each pastry case and bake in a preheated oven, 200°C (400°F), Gas Mark 6, for 15 minutes. Remove the foil and bake for a further 5 minutes. Reduce the oven temperature to 160°C (325°F), Gas Mark 3.

3 Beat the eggs, egg yolks, caster sugar and vanilla paste or extract together in a bowl. Heat the cream and milk in a saucepan until it is bubbling around the edges, then pour it over the egg mixture, stirring. Strain the custard into a jug and carefully pour into the pastry cases. Bake in the oven for about 20 minutes or until the custard is only just set. Let the tarts cool in the tin and serve dusted with icing sugar.

MAKES 12

1 tablespoon Vanilla Sugar (see page 168)

½ teaspoon ground cinnamon

double quantity Sweet Pastry (see page 71)

plain flour, for dusting

3 eggs

2 egg yolks

2 tablespoons caster sugar

1 teaspoon vanilla paste or ½ teaspoon vanilla extract

325 ml (11 fl oz) double cream

150 ml (¼ pint) milk

icing sugar, for dusting

chocolate

Chocolate bread and butter pudding

SERVES 6

200 g (7 oz) plain chocolate, broken into pieces

50 g (2 oz) unsalted butter, plus extra for greasing

½ teaspoon ground mixed spice

250 g (8 oz) brioche, cut into thin slices

3 eggs

25 g (1 oz) caster sugar

600 ml (1 pint) milk

cocoa powder or icing sugar, for dusting

single cream, to serve

I should think quite a few of you have already tried a chocolate version of this classic. This one uses brioche, which soaks up all of the cream and all of that chocolate to make an incredibly good bowl full.

1 Grease 6 individual ramekins or a 1.8 litre (3 pint) shallow ovenproof dish. Put the chocolate, half the butter and the mixed spice in a heatproof bowl set over a saucepan of barely simmering water so that the base of the bowl is not touching the water and leave until melted. Stir lightly.

2 Arrange about one-third of the brioche slices in the prepared ramekins or dish. Place spoonfuls of the chocolate sauce over the brioche. Cover with another third of the brioche slices and then the remaining sauce. Arrange the rest of the brioche on top.

3 Melt the remaining butter in a small saucepan, then beat into the eggs, caster sugar and milk in a bowl. Pour over the brioche and leave to stand for 30 minutes.

4 Bake in a preheated oven, 180°C (350°F), Gas Mark 4, for about 50 minutes or until the crust is golden. Dust the pudding liberally with cocoa powder or icing sugar and serve with single cream.

Gregg's tip

Cinnamon bread or fruited teabread can be used instead of the brioche.

Chocolate and chestnut cake

SERVES 6

butter, for greasing

250 g (8 oz) cooked peeled chestnuts

75 g (3 oz) plain chocolate, broken into pieces

2 tablespoons water

2 teaspoons brandy

4 eggs, separated

200 g (7 oz) caster sugar

FILLING AND TOPPING

300 ml (½ pint) double cream, whipped

1 marron glacé, cut into pieces

I do enjoy a good slice of cake – I know you can't hear me but in my mind I'm wearing a cardigan and sounding just like Mr Kipling. I'm almost growling at the thought of this slightly gooey chestnut texture with a big hit of cocoa flavour. Yum.

1 Line the bases of two 20 cm (8 inch) round sandwich tins and grease the sides. Purée the chestnuts in a blender or food processor until fairly smooth, adding a little water if necessary.

2 Put the chocolate with the water in a heatproof bowl set over a saucepan of barely simmering water so that the base of the bowl is not touching the water and leave until melted. Stir in the brandy.

3 Whisk the egg yolks and half the sugar together in a bowl using a hand-held electric whisk until thick enough to leave a trail when the whisk is lifted. Whisk in the warm chocolate mixture and the puréed chestnuts.

4 Whisk the egg whites in a large, grease-free bowl until stiff, then whisk in the remaining sugar. Using a large metal spoon, fold the egg whites into the chestnut mixture.

5 Divide the mixture between the prepared tins and bake in a preheated oven, 180°C (350°F), Gas Mark 4, for 35–40 minutes. Leave to cool slightly in the tins, then ease the cakes out on to a wire rack and leave to cool completely.

6 Use half the whipped cream to sandwich the cooled cakes together. Spread more cream over the top of the cake. Decorate with the pieces of marron glacé and chill until ready to serve.

Chocolate roulade

A big but delicately soft chocolate and cream dessert. An off-white creamy spiral runs the length of this beauty – a perfect partner to the light chocolate sponge.

1 Line and grease a 20 x 30 cm (8 x 12 inch) Swiss roll tin. Put the chocolate with the water in a heatproof bowl set over a saucepan of barely simmering water so that the base of the bowl is not touching the water and leave until melted.

2 Whisk the egg yolks and half the caster sugar together in a bowl using a hand-held electric whisk until thick enough to leave a trail when the whisk is lifted. Whisk in the warm chocolate.

3 Whisk the egg whites in a large, grease-free bowl until stiff, then whisk in the remaining caster sugar. Using a large metal spoon, fold the egg whites into the chocolate mixture.

4 Turn the mixture into the prepared tin and bake in a preheated oven, 180°C (350°F), Gas Mark 4, for 25–30 minutes until firm.

5 Leave to cool for 5 minutes, then cover with a clean, damp tea towel and chill overnight. Carefully remove the cloth and turn the roulade on to a sheet of greaseproof paper sprinkled thickly with icing sugar. Peel away the paper.

6 Spread the whipped cream evenly over the roulade and roll up like a Swiss roll.

MAKES ONE 20 CM
(8 INCH) ROLL

butter, for greasing

150 g (5 oz) plain chocolate, broken into pieces

3 tablespoons water

4 eggs, separated

150 g (5 oz) caster sugar

TO FINISH

icing sugar, for sprinkling

300 ml (½ pint) double cream, whipped

Chocolate fudge cake

This stunning cake is definitely one for the grown-ups. I have to be honest, it does take a bit of work but like all good things it is well worth it. When you slice through that chocolate topping to find the yummy layers below, you'll be glad you made the effort.

1 To make the cake, grease and line a 20 cm (8 inch) round cake tin. Mix the milk and lemon juice together. Put the chocolate in a heatproof bowl set over a saucepan of barely simmering water so that the base of the bowl is not touching the water and leave until melted.

2 Beat the butter and caster sugar together in a large bowl until pale and fluffy. Add the eggs and beat in. Sift the flour, bicarbonate of soda and cocoa powder into the bowl and mix well. Add half the milk mixture and beat well. Stir in the melted chocolate and remaining milk mixture and beat until smooth. Turn into the prepared tin and level the surface.

3 Bake in a preheated oven, 160°C (325°F), Gas Mark 3, for 1¼–1½ hours or until well risen and a skewer inserted into the centre comes out clean. Leave to cool in the tin.

4 Split the cake horizontally into 3 layers. Lightly whip the cream and stir in the praline. Use to sandwich the layers of cake together. Place on a serving plate.

5 To make the icing, put the chocolate and butter in a heatproof bowl set over a saucepan of barely simmering water so that the base of the bowl is not touching the water and leave until melted. Stir once. Remove the bowl from the pan. Add the icing sugar and milk and beat until smooth. Leave the icing until cool enough to hold its shape.

6 Using a palette knife, spread the icing all over the top and side of the cake.

SERVES 14–16

CAKE

250 ml (8 fl oz) milk

1 tablespoon freshly squeezed lemon juice

125 g (4 oz) plain chocolate, broken into pieces

125 g (4 oz) unsalted butter, plus extra for greasing

250 g (8 oz) caster sugar

2 eggs

300 g (10 oz) self-raising flour

1 teaspoon bicarbonate of soda

2 tablespoons cocoa powder

FILLING

150 ml (¼ pint) double cream

1 quantity Almond Praline (see page 184)

ICING

250 g (8 oz) plain chocolate, broken into pieces

125 g (4 oz) unsalted butter

200 g (7 oz) icing sugar, sifted, plus extra for dusting

5 tablespoons milk

melted plain chocolate, to decorate

Chocolate truffle gâteau

SERVES 12

butter, for greasing

4 eggs

100 g (3½ oz) caster sugar

100 g (3½ oz) plain flour

FILLING

450 ml (¾ pint) double cream

175 g (6 oz) milk chocolate, chopped

450 ml (¾ pint) Greek yogurt

175 g (6 oz) white chocolate, chopped

175 g (6 oz) plain chocolate, chopped

cocoa powder, for dusting

This is a wonderful layered lovely. It's sweet, but with a slightly sour aftertaste. You will have no problem making it, but you will be guaranteed to have an issue allowing it to set without eating it first.

1 Grease and line the base of a 23 cm (9 inch) loose-bottomed or springform cake tin. Whisk the eggs and sugar together in a bowl using a hand-held electric whisk until thick enough to leave a trail when the whisk is lifted.

2 Sift the flour into the bowl and fold in using a large metal spoon. Turn into the prepared tin and bake in a preheated oven, 190°C (375°F), Gas Mark 5 for about 15 minutes until risen and just firm to the touch. Transfer to a wire rack and leave to cool.

3 Clean the tin and line the side with fresh paper. Cut the sponge in half horizontally. Lay one half in the tin.

4 To make the filling, bring 150 ml (¼ pint) of the cream to the boil in a small saucepan. Remove from the heat and stir in the milk chocolate until melted. Turn into a bowl and stir in 150 ml (¼ pint) of the yogurt until smooth. Spoon the mixture over the sponge in the tin, spreading until level. Chill for about 30 minutes until beginning to set.

5 Using another 150 ml (¼ pint) of the cream and yogurt, and the white chocolate, make a second chocolate layer and spread over the milk chocolate. Chill for about 30 minutes until just setting.

6 Use the remaining cream, yogurt and plain chocolate to make a third layer and spread over the white chocolate. Cover with the remaining sponge and chill for 2–3 hours.

7 Remove the gâteau from the tin and transfer to a serving plate, peeling away the paper. Dust the top of the cake with cocoa powder.

White chocolate gâteau

I am a big fan of white chocolate – I'm not related to the Milky Bar kid you understand but I had to lick my lips at this recipe. I once had something very similar at Le Caprice and that sweet memory lingers still after all these years. I can't swear that this is exactly the same but it's pretty darn close!

1 Grease and line the bases of two 20 cm (8 inch) round sandwich tins. Whisk the eggs and caster sugar together in a large bowl using a hand-held electric whisk until thick enough to leave a trail when the whisk is lifted.

2 Sift the flour into the bowl. Add the grated chocolate and fold in using a large metal spoon.

3 Divide the mixture between the prepared tins and bake in a preheated oven, 180°C (350°F), Gas Mark 4, for 20–25 minutes until just firm to the touch. Transfer to a wire rack to cool.

4 Stir the rose essence into the crème fraîche and use to sandwich the 2 cakes together on a serving plate.

5 Put the white chocolate and butter in a heatproof bowl set over a saucepan of barely simmering water so that the base of the bowl is not touching the water and leave until melted. Allow to cool, then stir in the cream and icing sugar and beat until smooth. Leave the mixture to cool further until it forms soft peaks, then spread over the top and side of the cake using a palette knife.

6 Decorate the top of the cake with white chocolate curls, sugared rose petals, if you like, and a light dusting of icing sugar.

Gregg's tip

The sugared rose petals decorating this cake enhance the subtle rosewater flavouring. To make, lightly brush fresh rose petals with beaten egg white and dust them with caster sugar. Leave to dry on nonstick greaseproof paper for 1–2 hours before using.

SERVES 12

butter, for greasing

4 eggs

125 g (4 oz) caster sugar

125 g (4 oz) plain flour

50 g (2 oz) white chocolate, finely grated

TO FINISH

2–3 drops rose essence

150 ml (¼ pint) crème fraîche

200 g (7 oz) white chocolate, broken into pieces

75 g (3 oz) unsalted butter

3 tablespoons single cream, at room temperature

125 g (4 oz) icing sugar

white chocolate curls

sugared rose petals (optional)

icing sugar, for dusting

Chocolate gâteau with rum and walnuts

SERVES 6–8

CAKE

175 g (6 oz) butter

175 g (6 oz) caster sugar

3 large eggs

1 tablespoon rum

100 g (3½ oz) self-raising flour sifted with ½ teaspoon baking powder or plain flour with 1½ teaspoons baking powder

40 g (1½ oz) walnuts, finely chopped

40 g (1½ oz) digestive biscuits, crushed

FILLING AND TOPPING

75 g (3 oz) sultanas

3 tablespoons rum

175 g (6 oz) plain or bitter chocolate

150 g (5 oz) icing sugar, sifted

150 g (5 oz) butter

50 g (2 oz) walnuts, coarsely chopped

I know I shouldn't have favourites, I know I shouldn't but I'm only human. I ask you – a combination of walnuts, rum and chocolate: it's a heavenly mix. When you add to this digestive biscuits and sultanas you are putting together some of Gregg's favourite ingredients of all time into one gâteau.

1 To make the cake, line a 1 kg (2½ lb) loaf tin. Beat the butter and caster sugar together in a bowl until pale and fluffy. Beat the eggs with the rum, then gradually beat into the butter mixture, adding a little flour and baking powder if the mixture shows signs of curdling. When all the eggs and rum have been incorporated, add the remaining flour, the nuts and biscuit crumbs.

2 Spoon the mixture into the prepared tin and bake in a preheated oven, 180°C (350°F), Gas Mark 4, for about 45 minutes or until firm to the touch. Meanwhile, soak the sultanas in the rum for the filling and topping.

3 Leave the cake to cool in the tin for about 10 minutes, then turn out on to a wire rack and leave to cool completely. Split horizontally into 3 layers.

4 Break 150 g (5 oz) of the chocolate into pieces, put in a heatproof bowl set over a saucepan of barely simmering water so that the base of the bowl is not touching the water and leave until melted. Coarsely grate the remainder. Beat the icing sugar and butter together in a bowl. Add the melted chocolate and beat until light in texture. Add the sultanas, rum and half the walnuts.

5 Sandwich the layers together with some of the chocolate and rum mixture. Spread the remainder over the top but not the sides of the gâteau. Sprinkle the last of the walnuts and the grated chocolate over the top of the icing. Chill well before serving.

White chocolate fondue

SERVES 2

250 g (8 oz) white chocolate, grated

125 ml (4 fl oz) double cream

1 tablespoon kirsch (optional)

TO SERVE

fresh strawberries, hulled and halved if large

kiwifruit, peeled and cut into chunks

Very nice idea this and hours of fun for all the family; simply leave out the kirsch if you're involving the kids. You could use any soft fruit – it's a fantastic way of getting your kids to eat vitamin-packed fruit so choose whatever is in season.

1 Fill a fondue pot one-third full with water. Place the porcelain liner in the pot and add the chocolate and cream. Heat gently on the hob, stirring constantly, but do not allow it to boil. Alternatively, put the chocolate and cream in a heatproof bowl set over a saucepan of barely simmering water so that the base of the bowl is not touching the water. When the chocolate has melted, stir in the kirsch, if using.

2 Transfer the fondue pot or bowl to the table and keep warm over a burner. Serve with strawberries and chunks of kiwifruit, using bamboo skewers to dip the fruit into the fondue.

Fruit and chocolate fondue

I do love this fondue dipping. Fruit and Madeira cake along with apricot is a fine trio to stick in chocolate. But I can't help thinking a marshmallow could happily sneak in here, too.

1 Fill the fondue pot one-third full with water. Place the porcelain liner in the pot and heat on the hob. Alternatively, set a heatproof bowl over a saucepan of barely simmering water so that the base of the bowl is not touching the water. Pour the cream into the pot or bowl and heat gently. As soon as the cream starts to bubble around the edges, turn off the heat and whisk in the chocolate. When the chocolate has melted, add the vanilla extract and stir well to mix.

2 Transfer the fondue pot or bowl to the table and keep warm over a burner. Serve with cubes of cake, strawberries and slices of fresh or crystallized apricot, using fondue forks, cocktail sticks or bamboo skewers to dip the cake and fruit into the fondue.

SERVES 6–8

125 ml (4 fl oz) double cream

250 g (8 oz) plain chocolate, finely chopped

1 teaspoon vanilla extract

TO SERVE

cubes of sponge or Madeira cake

fresh strawberries, hulled and halved if large

slices of peeled fresh apricot or crystallized apricot

White chocolate cherry tart

SERVES 6–8

PASTRY

175 g (6 oz) plain flour, plus extra for dusting

½ teaspoon ground cinnamon

125 g (4 oz) unsalted butter, chilled and diced

25 g (1 oz) caster sugar

2–3 teaspoons iced water

FILLING

2 eggs

40 g (1½ oz) caster sugar

150 g (5 oz) white chocolate, finely chopped

300 ml (½ pint) double cream

450 g (1 lb) fresh black or red dessert cherries or 2 x 425 g (14 oz) cans pitted black or red cherries

ground cinnamon, for dusting

extra cherries, to decorate (optional)

Yeah! White chocolate and cherry is a fantastic combination. Sweet, almost wine-like, cherry juice against sugary white chocolate encased in a cinnamon pastry. Delicious!

1 To make the pastry, sift the flour and cinnamon into a bowl. Add the butter and rub in with your fingertips until the mixture resembles fine breadcrumbs. Stir in the sugar and add enough of the water to mix to a firm dough.

2 Turn the dough out on to a lightly floured surface and knead briefly. Wrap in foil and chill for 30 minutes.

3 Roll the dough out on a lightly floured surface and use to line a 23 x 2.5 cm (9 x 1 inch) deep loose-bottomed flan tin. Trim off the excess pastry around the rim. Line the tart case with foil, fill with baking beans and bake in a preheated oven, 200°C (400°F), Gas Mark 6, for 10 minutes. Remove the foil and beans and bake for a further 5 minutes. Reduce the oven temperature to 180°C (350°F), Gas Mark 4.

4 Meanwhile, to make the filling, beat the eggs and sugar together in a bowl. Put the chocolate in a heatproof bowl. Heat the cream in a small, heavy-based saucepan, then pour over the chocolate and stir until the chocolate has melted. Pour over the egg mixture, stirring constantly.

5 Pit the cherries, if using fresh, or thoroughly drain the canned cherries. Arrange in the flan case. Pour the chocolate mixture over the cherries.

6 Bake in the oven for about 45 minutes until the chocolate cream is set. Dust with cinnamon and serve warm, decorated with extra cherries if you like.

Gregg's tip

For a dark chocolate version, replace 5 g (¼ oz) of the flour in the pastry with 5 g (¼ oz) cocoa powder. In the filling, use finely chopped plain chocolate instead of white and use an extra 25 g (1 oz) caster sugar.

Chocolate meringue cream slice

MAKES ONE 30 CM
(12 INCH) SLICE

75 g (3 oz) plain flour

2 teaspoons baking
powder

pinch of salt

2½ tablespoons cocoa
powder

125 g (4 oz) butter, plus
extra for greasing

250 g (8 oz) caster sugar

2 large eggs, separated

6 tablespoons milk

100 g (3½ oz) flaked
almonds

TO FINISH

300 ml (½ pint) double
cream

50 g (2 oz) plain chocolate,
melted

This is absolutely fantastic – I kid you not. I would never
have dreamed of adding chocolate to a meringue but I
have to say it's a winning formula. Especially when you
add whipped cream – I could dive into this head first.

1 Line and grease a 20 x 30 cm (8 x 12 inch) rectangular baking tin.
Sift the flour, baking powder, salt and cocoa powder together into
a bowl. Beat the butter and half the sugar together in a separate
bowl until pale and fluffy, then beat in the egg yolks. Fold in the
flour mixture, then add the milk. Mix thoroughly and spread thinly
in the prepared tin.

2 Whisk the egg whites in a grease-free bowl until stiff, then
gradually whisk in the remaining sugar. Spread over the cake
mixture and sprinkle with the almonds.

3 Bake in a preheated oven, 180°C (350°F), Gas Mark 4, for
20 minutes. Leave to cool on a wire rack. Peel off the paper and
cut the cake in half lengthways. Slide one half on to a serving
plate, chocolate-side up, and spread with the whipped cream.
Top with the remaining cake, chocolate-side down. Drizzle the
melted chocolate across the top of the meringue.

Chocolate pancake stack with rum butter

It doesn't mess about this one. When we say rum we mean it. It just works: the heat from the boozy butter oozing over a stack of chocolate pancakes is a thing to behold.

1 To make the rum butter, beat the butter in a bowl until soft and creamy. Add the icing sugar and the rum and beat together until light and creamy. Transfer to a serving dish.

2 To make the pancakes, sift the flour, cocoa powder and baking powder into a bowl. Stir in the caster sugar. Make a well in the centre and add the egg and a little of the milk to the well. Whisk the mixture to make a stiff batter, then beat in the remaining milk. Stir in the chocolate, sultanas and almonds.

3 Heat a little oil in a large frying pan or griddle pan. Take spoonfuls of the batter, making sure you scoop up some fruit, nuts and chocolate each time, and spoon into the pan. Fry gently until just firm and browned on the underside. Turn the pancakes over and cook on the other side for a further 1 minute. Remove and keep warm while cooking the remainder, adding more oil to the pan as necessary.

4 To serve, stack the pancakes and top with spoonfuls of the rum butter.

Variations

White or plain chocolate, grated orange or walnuts are equally good in the pancakes, and brandy or an orange-flavoured liqueur can be used instead of rum in the butter.

SERVES 4–6

RUM BUTTER

75 g (3 oz) unsalted butter, softened

50 g (2 oz) icing sugar

3 tablespoons rum

PANCAKES

100 g (3½ oz) self-raising flour

15 g (½ oz) cocoa powder

½ teaspoon baking powder

25 g (1 oz) caster sugar

1 egg, beaten

175 ml (6 fl oz) milk

125 g (4 oz) milk chocolate, roughly chopped

25 g (1 oz) sultanas

25 g (1 oz) flaked almonds

oil, for shallow-frying

Triple chocolate brûlée

SERVES 6

8 egg yolks

125 g (4 oz) caster sugar

600 ml (1 pint) double cream

125 g (4 oz) plain chocolate, finely chopped

125 g (4 oz) white chocolate, finely chopped

125 g (4 oz) milk chocolate, finely chopped

3 tablespoons Amaretto di Saronno or brandy (optional)

This is brilliantly clever – you don't even have to bake these little beauties. Triple chocolate with the marzipan flavour of Amaretto is shockingly good. These have got to become one of your dinner party standbys.

1 Mix the egg yolks and half the sugar together in a bowl with a fork. Pour the cream into a saucepan and bring almost to the boil. Gradually beat the cream into the yolk mixture.

2 Strain the custard into a measuring jug, then divide it equally between 3 bowls. Stir a different chocolate into each bowl of hot custard, adding a tablespoon of the Amaretto or brandy to each, if using. Stir until melted.

3 Divide the plain chocolate custard between 6 ramekins. When cool, transfer the dishes to the freezer for 10 minutes to chill and set.

4 Take the dishes out of the freezer, stir the white chocolate custard and spoon it over the dark layer in the dishes. Return to the freezer for 10 minutes.

5 Take the dishes out of the freezer, stir the milk chocolate custard and spoon it into the dishes. Chill the custards in the refrigerator for 3–4 hours until set. About 25 minutes before serving, sprinkle the tops of the dishes with the remaining sugar and caramelize with a blowtorch. Leave at room temperature until ready to eat.

Baked chocolate soufflé

sunflower oil, for oiling

25 g (1 oz) cocoa powder

40 g (1½ oz) cornflour

300 ml (½ pint) milk

50 g (2 oz) caster sugar

50 g (2 oz) butter

4 eggs, separated

1 teaspoon vanilla extract

25 g (1 oz) icing sugar, sifted, to serve

I understand people get nervous when you mention soufflé but I promise you if you just follow these instructions you will be absolutely fine. Trust me, the recipe works very well. You too can be a soufflé wizard!

1 Oil a 1.2 litre (2 pint) soufflé dish. Blend the cocoa powder and cornflour with a little of the milk in a saucepan. Add the remaining milk, the caster sugar and butter and cook, stirring, until thickened. Leave to cool slightly, then beat in the egg yolks, one at a time, and the vanilla extract.

2 Whisk the egg whites in a large, grease-free bowl until stiff. Using a large metal spoon, fold about 2 tablespoons of the egg whites into the chocolate mixture to loosen, then carefully fold in the remainder.

3 Turn into the prepared soufflé dish and bake immediately in a preheated oven, 180°C (350°F), Gas Mark 4, for 35–40 minutes until risen and firm on top.

4 Sprinkle with the icing sugar and serve immediately.

Hot chocolate liqueur soufflé

Soufflé and sauce? It is a teensy bit extravagant isn't it, but it's a proper grown-ups' dessert. Very elegant, very impressive-looking and a great way to show off your culinary skills.

1 Grease an 18 cm (7 inch) soufflé dish and sprinkle with caster sugar to coat. Put the butter, flour and milk in a saucepan and heat gently, stirring constantly, until boiling. Stir vigorously until a thick paste is formed. Cook for 2–3 minutes, still stirring.

2 Remove from the heat, add the chocolate and stir until melted and completely blended into the mixture. Beat in the liqueur and egg yolks.

3 Whisk all the egg whites in a large, grease-free bowl until very stiff, then add the caster sugar. Whisk again until very stiff. Using a large metal spoon, carefully fold the chocolate mixture into the egg whites.

4 Pour the mixture into the prepared soufflé dish and bake in a preheated oven, 180°C (350°F), Gas Mark 4, for 45–50 minutes until well risen. Do not open the oven door.

5 Meanwhile, to make the sauce, pour the cream into a small saucepan and add the chocolate. Heat gently, stirring constantly, until the chocolate has melted and is thoroughly smooth. Do not boil. Stir in the liqueur and egg yolk. Pour into a jug.

6 To serve, dust the soufflé with icing sugar and take it directly from the oven to a heatproof mat on the table. Serve the soufflé with the sauce.

SERVES 4

50 g (2 oz) butter, plus extra for greasing

50 g (2 oz) plain flour

300 ml (½ pint) milk

75 g (3 oz) plain dark or white chocolate, broken into pieces

2 tablespoons crème de menthe

3 eggs, separated, plus 1 egg white

50 g (2 oz) caster sugar, plus extra for sprinkling

icing sugar, for dusting

SAUCE

150 ml (¼ pint) double cream

50 g (2 oz) plain or white chocolate, broken into pieces

2 tablespoons crème de menthe

1 egg yolk

Chocolate steamed puddings

This for me just brings back very happy childhood memories. This was my absolute favourite pudding at school. In fact it could be this that started my great pudding love affair in the first place. You can serve it with whatever you want but if you're doing it for me – I'm having the custard, thanks mum.

1 Beat the butter with the brown sugar in a bowl until pale and fluffy. Add the eggs gradually, beating well after each addition. Stir in the melted chocolate together with the flour, baking powder and milk until well blended. Spoon or pipe the mixture into 6 medium or 8 small dariole moulds so that they are just three-quarters full.

2 Cover the moulds loosely with foil and steam over a pan of gently simmering water for about 40 minutes, until set. Serve warm with cream or custard.

SERVES 6–8

150 g (5 oz) softened butter

150 g (5 oz) soft dark brown sugar

2 eggs, beaten

50 g (2 oz) bitter chocolate, melted and cooled

110 g (3¾ oz) plain flour

½ teaspoon baking powder

25 ml (1 fl oz) milk

cream or custard, to serve

Chocolate puddle pudding

SERVES 5–6

250 g (8 oz) plain chocolate, broken into pieces

300 ml (½ pint) milk

2 tablespoons brandy (optional)

50 g (2 oz) unsalted butter, softened

150 g (5 oz) caster sugar

2 eggs, separated

25 g (1 oz) self-raising flour

25 g (1 oz) cocoa powder, plus extra for dusting

whipped cream, to serve

Is this clever or what? You mix it all together, stick it in the oven and when it comes out it's got a light crusted sponge on top and a hot sticky chocolate sauce underneath. Quite brilliant.

1 Put the chocolate in a small saucepan with the milk and heat gently until the chocolate has melted. Stir in the brandy, if using.

2 Beat together the butter and sugar in a bowl until fluffy. Gradually beat in the egg yolks, flour, cocoa powder and chocolate mixture.

3 Whisk the egg whites in a separate, grease-free bowl until they hold their shape. Using a large metal spoon, fold a quarter of the egg whites into the chocolate mixture. Fold in the remaining egg whites.

4 Turn the mixture into a 1.5 litre (2½ pint) pie dish and place in a roasting tin. Pour boiling water to a depth of 2.5 cm (1 inch) into the tin. Bake in a preheated oven, 180°C (350°F), Gas Mark 4, for about 35 minutes until a crust has formed.

5 Dust the pudding generously with cocoa powder and serve hot with whipped cream.

Devil's chocolate food cake

If you have a sweet tooth like me you will be in heaven. It is rich and it is sweet. Good dark cake with a marshmallowy snow white frosting all over it – good heavens.

1 Line the base and grease a 20 cm (8 inch) round, deep straight-sided cake tin. Put the chocolate, butter, brown sugar and syrup in a saucepan and heat gently until just melted. Leave to cool.

2 Sift the flour, cocoa powder and bicarbonate of soda into a bowl. Make a well in the centre, add the cooled melted ingredients to the well and stir in. Stir in the eggs and beat well, then mix in the milk.

3 Pour the mixture into the prepared tin and bake in a preheated oven, 180°C (350°F), Gas Mark 4, for 30 minutes or until set. Leave to cool for a few minutes in the tin before turning out on to a wire rack to cool completely.

4 While the cake is cooling, to make the frosting, put the granulated sugar and water in a heavy-based saucepan and heat gently, without stirring, until the sugar has dissolved. Bring to the boil and boil, without stirring, until a sugar thermometer registers 114°C (240°F). Just before this temperature is reached, whisk the egg white in a grease-free bowl until stiff. Remove the syrup from the heat and when the bubbles have subsided, pour the syrup in a thin stream on to the egg white, whisking constantly. When the frosting is thick and opaque, add your chosen flavouring.

5 Working quickly before it sets, coat the top and side of the cake with the frosting, swirling it with a palette knife. Leave the frosting to set, then lightly dust the top of the cake with a little cocoa powder.

MAKES ONE 20 CM (8 INCH) CAKE

125 g (4 oz) plain chocolate, broken into pieces

150 g (5 oz) butter, plus extra for greasing

125 g (4 oz) soft dark brown sugar

1 tablespoon golden syrup

200 g (7 oz) plain flour

15 g (1 oz) cocoa powder, plus extra for dusting

1 teaspoon bicarbonate of soda

2 eggs, beaten

125 ml (4 fl oz) milk

AMERICAN FROSTING

250 g (8 oz) granulated sugar

125 ml (4 fl oz) water

1 egg white

a few drops of vanilla extract, 1 teaspoon coffee essence or 1 teaspoon freshly squeezed lemon juice

Chocolate pots

SERVES 4

75 g (3 oz) plain chocolate, broken into pieces

25 g (1 oz) butter

1 tablespoon double cream

3 eggs, separated

1 tablespoon chocolate- or coffee-flavoured liqueur

TO DECORATE

whipped cream

crystallized violet petals (optional)

Everybody should know how to make these – they are a dinner party must. They look divine and you can make them well in advance so you get more time to spend with your guests.

1 Put the chocolate and butter in a heatproof bowl set over a saucepan of barely simmering water so that the base of the bowl is not touching the water and leave until melted. Remove the bowl from the pan and beat in the cream and the egg yolks, then stir in the liqueur.

2 Whisk the egg whites in a large, grease-free bowl until stiff. Using a large metal spoon, fold the egg whites into the chocolate mixture. Spoon into 4 coffee cups or small glasses and chill until set.

3 Just before serving, top each pot with a rosette of whipped cream and decorate with crystallized violets, if you like. Serve immediately.

Profiteroles

Soft light choux pastry filled with cream, with chocolate sauce poured over the top. My son Tom would walk over hot coals for a plate of good profiteroles.

1 Dampen a baking sheet with water. Put the choux pastry dough into a piping bag fitted with a plain 1 cm (½ inch) nozzle and pipe small mounds on to the prepared baking sheet.

2 Bake in a preheated oven, 220°C (425°F), Gas Mark 7, for 10 minutes. Reduce the heat to 190°C (375°F), Gas Mark 5, and bake for a further 20–25 minutes until golden.

3 Meanwhile, to make the sauce, put the chocolate, 2 tablespoons of the water and the coffee in a small saucepan and heat gently until the chocolate has melted. Add the remaining water and the caster sugar and heat gently, stirring, until the sugar has dissolved, then simmer, uncovered, for 10 minutes. Leave to cool.

4 When cooked, make a slit in the side of each profiterole and leave to cool on a wire rack. To make the filling, whip the cream in a bowl until stiff, then fold in the icing sugar and vanilla extract. Pipe or spoon a little into each profiterole. Pile the profiteroles on a serving dish.

SERVES 4–6

1 quantity Choux Pastry (see page 177)

CHOCOLATE SAUCE

175 g (6 oz) plain chocolate, broken into pieces

150 ml (½ pint) water

1 teaspoon instant coffee powder

125 g (4 oz) caster sugar

FILLING

175 ml (6 fl oz) double cream

1 tablespoon icing sugar, sifted

2–3 drops of vanilla extract

Chocolate mousse tartlets

It's easier eating a small pudding. Just tell yourself it's only a little bit. Good pastry, light chocolate inside with just a hint of grown-up booze. Lovely.

1 Sift the flour into a bowl. Add the butter and rub in with your fingertips until the mixture resembles fine breadcrumbs. Stir in the caster sugar, then add the egg and mix to a firm dough, adding a little iced water if necessary.

2 Turn the dough out on a lightly floured surface and knead briefly. Roll out and use to line four deep 7.5 cm (3 inch) tartlet tins. Re-roll the trimmings and line 2 more tartlet tins. Press a square of foil into each and place the tins on a baking sheet. Bake in a preheated oven, 200°C (400°F), Gas Mark 6, for 15 minutes. Remove the foil and bake the tartlet cases for a further 5 minutes. Leave to cool.

3 To make the filling, put the chocolate with the water in a heatproof bowl set over a saucepan of barely simmering water so that the base of the bowl is not touching the water and leave until melted, stirring occasionally.

4 Remove the bowl from the pan and stir in the butter until it has melted. Add the brandy or Cointreau and stir in the egg yolks. Whisk the egg whites in a grease-free bowl until they are stiff and dry. Using a large metal spoon, fold the egg whites into the chocolate mixture.

5 Spoon the mousse mixture into the tartlet cases, then transfer to the refrigerator for 2–3 hours until set. Dust the tartlets lightly with icing sugar before serving. Serve cold.

MAKES 6

125 g (4 oz) plain flour, plus extra for dusting

50 g (2 oz) butter, chilled and diced

25 g (1 oz) caster sugar

1 small egg, beaten

icing sugar, for dusting

FILLING

75 g (3 oz) plain chocolate, broken into pieces

1 tablespoon water

5 g (¼ oz) unsalted butter

1 teaspoon brandy or Cointreau

2 small eggs, separated

Double chocolate brownies

MAKES 14–16

375 g (12 oz) white chocolate

50 g (2 oz) unsalted butter, plus extra for greasing

250 g (8 oz) plain chocolate

3 eggs

150 g (5 oz) caster sugar

175 g (6 oz) self-raising flour

1 teaspoon almond essence

150 g (5 oz) broken walnuts

I've only got to hear the word double chocolate and I go weak at the knees! Serve warm with ice cream and an indulgent snack instantly becomes a decadent dessert.

1 Grease and line a 28 x 20 cm (11 x 8 inch) shallow baking tin. Break up 125 g (4 oz) of the white chocolate and put in a heatproof bowl with the butter. Set over a saucepan of barely simmering water so that the base of the bowl is not touching the water and leave until melted. Stir lightly. Roughly chop the remaining white chocolate and the plain chocolate.

2 Whisk the eggs and sugar together in a large bowl until foamy. Beat in the melted chocolate mixture. Sift the flour into the bowl and stir it into the mixture with the almond essence, walnuts and chopped white and plain chocolate.

3 Turn the brownie mixture into the prepared tin and bake in a preheated oven, 190°C (375°F), Gas Mark 5, for 35 minutes until risen and just firm. Leave to cool in the tin.

4 Turn out of the tin on to a board and cut into squares or rectangles.

Chocolate cheesecake

I like this as it has a touch of the unusual – no one expects a dark cheesecake do they? It's quite a remarkable dessert. It holds firm when you slice it but it tastes much lighter than it looks. All without losing any of its intense chocolate flavour.

1 To make the biscuit case, grease a 23 cm (9 inch) loose-bottomed flan tin. Process the biscuits in a food processor to fine crumbs. Melt the butter in a saucepan, add the biscuit crumbs and demerara sugar and mix well.

2 Press the crumb mixture over the base and side of the prepared tin. Chill the biscuit case until firm.

3 Put the chocolate in a heatproof bowl set over a saucepan of barely simmering water so that the base of the bowl is not touching the water and leave until melted. Beat the cream cheese, caster sugar and egg yolks together in a bowl, then stir in the chocolate. Lightly whip half the cream in a separate bowl and fold into the filling mixture.

4 Whisk the egg whites with the cream of tartar in a grease-free bowl until stiff. Using a large metal spoon, fold the egg whites into the filling mixture. Turn the filling into the biscuit case and chill until set.

5 Whip the remaining cream in a bowl until stiff enough to pipe. Decorate the cheesecake with the cream and chocolate curls.

Gregg's tip

To make chocolate curls, shave thin layers from a block of chocolate using a potato peeler.

SERVES 6–8

BISCUIT CASE

250 g (8 oz) digestive biscuits

75 g (2 oz) butter, plus extra for greasing

50 g (2 oz) demerara sugar

FILLING

175 g (6 oz) plain chocolate, broken into pieces

250 g (8 oz) cream cheese

75 g (3 oz) caster sugar

2 eggs, separated

300 ml (½ pint) double cream

¼ teaspoon cream of tartar

chocolate curls, to decorate

Chocoholic's Alaska

SERVES 10

SPONGE

50 g (2 oz) unsalted butter, softened, plus extra for greasing

50 g (2 oz) caster sugar

1 egg

40 g (1½ oz) self-raising flour, sifted

¼ teaspoon baking powder

15 g (½ oz) cocoa powder

2 tablespoons coffee-flavoured liqueur

TO FINISH

1 litre (1¾ pint) round tub chocolate ice cream

250 g (8 oz) plain chocolate, broken into pieces

75 g (3 oz) unsalted butter

4 egg whites

250 g (8 oz) caster sugar

A fair amount of work goes into this but the results are stunning – meringue on top of ice cream and sponge is a real feast. Don't cook anything else: invite people around and just serve this. They won't be disappointed!

1 To make the sponge, grease and line the base of an 18 cm (7 inch) round cake tin. Beat the butter, sugar, egg, flour, baking powder and cocoa powder together in a bowl. Turn into the prepared tin and level the surface. Bake in a preheated oven, 180°C (350°F), Gas Mark 4, for 20–25 minutes until just firm. Transfer to a wire rack to cool.

2 Cut the sponge in half horizontally and drizzle with the liqueur. Turn the ice cream out of the tub, keeping it in shape. Using a large knife, slice the block of ice cream in half horizontally. Put one sponge layer on a flat ovenproof serving plate. Alternatively, use the base of a 20 cm (8 inch) round loose-bottomed cake or flan tin so that you can lift it on to a decorative plate to serve.

3 Cover with one half of the ice cream. Cover this with the other half of the sponge, then the remaining ice cream. Trim off any excess sponge. Return to the freezer.

4 Put the chocolate and butter in a heatproof bowl set over a saucepan of barely simmering water so that the base of the bowl is not touching the water and stir lightly until melted and smooth. Quickly spread the chocolate mixture in a thin layer all over the ice cream and sponge. Return to the freezer.

5 Whisk the egg whites in a large, grease-free bowl until stiff. Gradually whisk in the sugar, a little at a time, until stiff and glossy. Spread the meringue over the chocolate sauce to cover. Make soft peaks over the meringue with the back of a spoon, then return to the freezer.

6 Transfer the Alaska to the refrigerator about 10 minutes before serving. Bake in a preheated oven, 230°C (450°F), Gas Mark 8, for 3–5 minutes until the meringue is turning golden. Serve immediately.

classic puddings

Sticky toffee pudding

SERVES 8

125 g (4 oz) chopped stoned dried dates

150 ml (¼ pint) water

125 g (4 oz) unsalted butter, softened, plus extra for greasing

100 g (3½ oz) caster sugar

2 teaspoons vanilla paste or 1 tablespoon vanilla extract

3 eggs

225 g (7½ oz) self-raising flour

1 teaspoon baking powder

ice cream, to serve (optional)

SAUCE

300 ml (½ pint) double cream, plus extra to serve (optional)

150 g (5 oz) soft light brown sugar

50 g (2 oz) butter

I love this. Who doesn't? It is one of the first puddings I ordered when I started going out to restaurants. Moist, fluffy sponge and toffee flavour that's so sweet it makes you smile.

1 Put the dates and water in a small saucepan and bring to the boil. Reduce the heat and simmer gently for 5 minutes until the dates are soft and pulpy. Purée using an immersion blender or transfer to a food processor or blender. Leave to cool.

2 Meanwhile, to make the sauce, put half the cream, brown sugar and butter in a small, heavy-based saucepan and heat gently until the sugar has dissolved. Bring to the boil, then let the sauce bubble for about 5 minutes until it turns to a rich, dark caramel. Stir in the remaining cream and set aside.

3 Grease and line the bases of 8 metal 150 ml (¼ pint) pudding moulds. Put the unsalted butter, caster sugar, vanilla paste, eggs, flour and baking powder in a bowl and beat with a hand-held electric whisk for 1–2 minutes until pale and creamy.

4 Stir the date purée into the pudding mixture and divide it between the prepared moulds. Level the tops and place the moulds in a roasting tin. Pour boiling water to a depth of 1.5 cm (¾ inch) into the tin and cover with foil. Bake the puddings in a preheated oven, 180°C (350°F), Gas Mark 4, for 35–40 minutes until they are risen and firm to the touch.

5 Leave the puddings in the moulds while you reheat the toffee sauce, then loosen the edges of the moulds and invert the puddings on to serving plates. Cover with plenty of the sauce and serve with extra cream or ice cream.

Bread and butter pudding

SERVES 4

40 g (1½ oz) butter

4 slices of white bread, crusts removed

75 g (3 oz) apricot jam (optional)

2 tablespoons chopped mixed peel

3 tablespoons sultanas

475 ml (16 fl oz) milk

2 tablespoons caster sugar

2 eggs, beaten

cream, to serve (optional)

An absolute classic. Really easy to make and I don't know anybody who doesn't like it. Slightly crispy on top and creamy and soft underneath.

1 Use 15 g (½ oz) of the butter to grease a 1.2 litre (2 pint) ovenproof serving dish. Spread the remaining butter over the bread, then spread with the jam, if using. Cut the bread into small triangles. Layer the bread in the dish, sprinkling the mixed peel and sultanas between the layers.

2 Put the milk and sugar in a saucepan and heat to just below boiling point. Whisk in the beaten eggs, then strain the mixture over the pudding. Leave to soak for 30 minutes.

3 Place the dish in a large roasting tin. Pour boiling water into the tin to come at least halfway up the sides of the dish. Bake in a preheated oven, 180°C (350°F), Gas Mark 4, for 45 minutes. Increase the oven temperature to 190°C (375°F), Gas Mark 5, and bake for a further 10–15 minutes or until crisp and golden on top and just set. Serve immediately, with cream, if you like.

Brown Betty

Quite simple but nonetheless absolutely yummy. I enjoy the sweet acidity of the apples but they are topped off to perfection by the sweetened bread.

1 Spread the bread thickly with the butter and cut each slice into 4. Grease a 1.5 litre (2½ pint) ovenproof dish generously and line with some of the bread, butter-side down.

2 Cover with half the apples, sprinkle with one-third of the sugar and arrange another layer of bread over the top. Cover with the remaining apples, sprinkle with another third of sugar and top with the remaining bread, butter-side up and slightly overlapping. Sprinkle with the remaining sugar.

3 Cover with foil and bake in a preheated oven, 180°C (350°F), Gas Mark 4, for 35 minutes. Remove the foil and bake for a further 5 minutes until crisp and golden. Serve hot with custard or cream.

SERVES 6

10 slices of white bread, crusts removed

75 g (3 oz) butter, plus extra for greasing

750 g–1 kg (1½–2 lb) cooking apples, such as Bramley, peeled, cored and sliced

75 g (3 oz) soft light brown sugar

custard (see page 170) or cream, to serve

Christmas pudding

SERVES 8–10

175 g (6 oz) plain flour

2 teaspoons ground mixed spice

1 teaspoon ground cinnamon

½ teaspoon freshly grated nutmeg

175 g (6 oz) fresh white breadcrumbs

175 g (6 oz) butter, diced, plus extra for greasing

175 g (6 oz) soft brown sugar

350 g (12 oz) sultanas

250 g (8 oz) raisins

250 g (8 oz) currants

75 g (3 oz) chopped mixed peel

finely grated rind and juice of 1 orange

2 eggs, beaten

125 ml (4 fl oz) brown ale

holly sprig, to decorate (optional)

TO SERVE

2–3 tablespoons brandy (optional)

cream or Brandy Butter (see page 173)

I had to include this – be careful if you are going to hide money inside it as people have been known to break teeth! My compliment of choice is brandy butter with whipped cream but it is of course entirely up to you.

1 Grease a 1.8 litre (3 pint) pudding basin. Sift the flour and spices into a bowl and stir in the breadcrumbs. Add the butter and rub in with your fingertips. Stir in the sugar, then add all the remaining ingredients and mix thoroughly.

2 Turn the mixture into the prepared pudding basin, cover with a pudding cloth or greaseproof paper and foil and steam for 6 hours, topping up the saucepan with boiling water as necessary.

3 Leave to cool slightly, then remove the cloth or paper and leave to cool completely. Cover with clean greaseproof paper and foil and store in a cool, dry place.

4 To serve, steam the pudding again for 2–2½ hours. Turn out on to a warmed serving dish. If you like, pour over 2–3 tablespoons warmed brandy and ignite. Top with a holly sprig to decorate and serve with cream or Brandy Butter.

Gregg's tip

If possible, make your Christmas pudding 3–4 months before Christmas to allow the mixture to mature.

Chestnut roulade

Don't be ashamed about showing off – it's ok when you're cooking. A roulade looks so sophisticated: large spirals and contrasting colours when you cut into it, with the added bonus that it's not difficult.

1 Line and grease a 20 x 30 cm (8 x 12 inch) Swiss roll tin. Whisk the egg yolks and caster sugar together in a bowl using a hand-held electric whisk until thick enough to leave a trail when the whisk is lifted. Beat the chestnut purée and orange juice together in a separate bowl until blended, then whisk into the egg mixture.

2 Whisk the egg whites in a large, grease-free bowl until stiff. Using a large metal spoon, fold the egg whites into the chestnut mixture.

3 Turn the mixture into the prepared tin and bake in a preheated oven, 180°C (350°F), Gas Mark 4, for 25–30 minutes until firm.

4 Leave to cool for 5 minutes, then cover with a clean, damp tea towel and leave until cold. Carefully turn the roulade on to a sheet of greaseproof paper sprinkled thickly with icing sugar. Peel away the paper.

5 Put the cream, orange rind and Grand Marnier in a bowl and whip until stiff. Spread over the roulade and roll up like a Swiss roll. Transfer to a serving dish.

MAKES ONE 30 CM (12 INCH) ROLL

butter, for greasing

3 eggs, separated

125 g (4 oz) caster sugar

250 g (8 oz) can unsweetened chestnut purée

finely grated rind and juice of 1 orange

icing sugar, for sprinkling

300 ml (½ pint) double cream

2 tablespoons Grand Marnier

Coffee and walnut gâteau

MAKES ONE 20 CM
(8 INCH) GÂTEAU

butter, for greasing

4 eggs

175 g (6 oz) caster sugar

125 g (4 oz) plain flour,
sifted

1 tablespoon vegetable oil

125 g (4 oz) walnuts, finely
chopped

1 quantity Coffee Butter
Cream (see page 173)

chopped walnuts,
to decorate

Coffee and walnut are both lovely deep flavours. I find this strangely comforting – I must also at this point confess my preference for brown-coloured puddings!

1 Line and grease two 20 cm (8 inch) round sandwich tins. Whisk the eggs and sugar together in a bowl using a hand-held electric whisk until thick enough to leave a trail when the whisk is lifted.

2 Partially fold in the flour, then add the oil and chopped walnuts and fold in gently. Divide between the prepared tins and bake in a preheated oven, 190°C (375°F), Gas Mark 5, for 35 minutes until the cakes spring back when lightly pressed. Turn out on to a wire rack to cool.

3 Spread half the butter cream over one of the cake rounds, lay the second cake round on top and spread with the remaining butter cream. Sprinkle with chopped walnuts to decorate.

Gregg's tip

If you want to be really fancy, slice each cake in half horizontally. Spread a quarter of the butter cream on to 3 of the cake rounds and sandwich them together. Cover the top and side of the cake with the remaining butter cream and decorate with chopped walnuts.

Black forest gâteau

SERVES 6

butter, for greasing

3 large eggs

75 g (3 oz) caster sugar

50 g (2 oz) plain flour

1 tablespoon cocoa powder

1 tablespoon vegetable oil

TO FINISH

425 g (14 oz) can black cherries

1 tablespoon arrowroot

3 tablespoons kirsch

300 ml (½ pint) double cream, whipped

plain chocolate curls (optional)

Black forest, black beauty. Layers of dark sponge with cream and the added delight of juicy cherries. I think now we can redefine this cake as truly retro – but still delicious.

1 Line and grease a 20 cm (8 inch) round cake tin. Whisk the eggs and sugar together in a bowl using a hand-held electric whisk until thick enough to leave a trail when the whisk is lifted. Sift the flour with the cocoa powder and fold into the egg mixture using a large metal spoon, then fold in the oil.

2 Turn into the prepared tin and bake in a preheated oven, 190°C (375°F), Gas Mark 5, for 30–35 minutes. Leave to cool on a wire rack.

3 Drain the cherries and mix a little of the juice with the arrowroot in a small bowl. Pour the remaining juice into a saucepan and bring to the boil. Pour on to the arrowroot mixture and stir well. Return to the pan and heat gently, stirring until thick and clear. Pit the cherries if necessary, add to the pan and leave to cool.

4 Slice the cake in half horizontally and sprinkle both layers with the kirsch. Place one layer on a serving plate and pipe a line of cream around the top edge. Spread the cherry mixture in the centre and top with the other layer.

5 Spread half the remaining cream around the side of the gâteau and press chocolate curls into it, if using. Pipe the remaining cream on top of the gâteau.

Speedy blackcurrant sponge pie

There are times when you need a speedy dessert. This recipe cuts a few corners but it still delivers a lovely pudding. Blackcurrants are great anyway: very pretty and a nice blend of sweet and sharp.

1 Grease a 23 cm (9 inch) fluted ceramic flan dish or tin. Mix the blackcurrants with the granulated sugar and put in the prepared dish or tin.

2 Put the butter, brown sugar, eggs, flour and baking powder in a large bowl. Using a wooden spoon, beat vigorously for about 2 minutes until soft and creamy. If using an electric mixer, beat for 1 minute only.

3 Spread the mixture over the blackcurrants, smooth the surface and sprinkle with the almonds. Bake in a preheated oven, 180°C (350°F), Gas Mark 4, for 40–45 minutes until the sponge topping is well risen, golden brown and cooked through. If necessary, cover with foil during baking to prevent over-browning. Serve hot or cold with vanilla ice cream, custard or cream.

SERVES 8

butter, for greasing

500 g (1 lb) blackcurrants, topped and tailed if fresh, defrosted if frozen

75 g (3 oz) granulated sugar

125 g (4 oz) soft butter

125 g (4 oz) soft light brown sugar

2 eggs

125 g (4 oz) self-raising flour, sifted

1 teaspoon baking powder

25 g (1 oz) flaked almonds

vanilla ice cream (see page 148), custard (see page 170) or cream, to serve

Butterscotch meringue pie

I love butterscotch. I think it's probably one of my favourite flavours in the world. Combined with a meringue top – I mean this is my idea of heaven!

1 Roll the pastry out on a lightly floured surface and use to line a 25 cm (10 inch) loose-bottomed fluted flan tin. Line the flan case with foil, fill with baking beans and bake in a preheated oven, 200°C (400°F), Gas Mark 6, for about 15 minutes until the pastry has begun to form a slight crust. Remove the foil and beans and bake for a further 10 minutes or until the pastry is dry and golden brown.

2 Melt the butter in a heavy-based saucepan until foaming. Add the brown sugar and stir well, then remove from the heat. Add the boiling water, shielding your hand in case the mixture spits, and stir well.

3 Blend the cornflour with a little of the milk to a smooth paste. Put the remaining milk in a saucepan and stir in the cornflour paste. Add the butter and sugar mixture. Bring to the boil over a gentle heat, stirring constantly. Reduce the heat and simmer for 1 minute, stirring. Leave to cool slightly.

4 Pour half the milk mixture on to the egg yolks in a bowl, beating constantly, then return the egg yolk mixture to the milk mixture in the pan and cook over a gentle heat for 2 minutes, stirring. Remove from the heat and pour into the flan case. Leave to cool completely.

5 Whisk the egg whites in a grease-free bowl until stiff, sprinkle over 40 g (1½ oz) of the caster sugar and whisk again until stiff and glossy. Lightly fold in the remaining sugar. Spoon the meringue evenly over the filling and peak, using the flat side of a knife.

6 Bake in a preheated oven, 150°C (300°F), Gas Mark 2, for 30 minutes until the meringue is set and lightly browned on top. Leave to cool before serving.

SERVES 8–10

double quantity Shortcrust Pastry (see page 176)

plain flour, for dusting

75 g (3 oz) butter

175 g (6 oz) soft dark brown sugar

200 ml (7 fl oz) boiling water

3 tablespoons cornflour

450 ml (¾ pint) milk

2 eggs, separated

75 g (3 oz) caster sugar

Pavlova

SERVES 6–8

4 egg whites

250 g (8 oz) caster sugar

1 tablespoon cornflour

2 teaspoons white wine vinegar

¼ teaspoon vanilla extract

FILLING

300 ml (½ pint) double cream

2 bananas, sliced

1 small pineapple, peeled, cored and cut into cubes

pulp from 2 passion fruit

2 peaches, peeled, stoned and sliced

This dish was actually named after a Russian ballet dancer. To this day the Australians and New Zealanders' still disagree over who invented it. I think it's great naming desserts after people. You ask my uncle Rice Pudding!

1 Line a baking sheet with silicone paper. Whisk the egg whites in a large, grease-free bowl until stiff. Add the sugar, a tablespoon at a time, whisking until the meringue is very stiff. Whisk in the cornflour, vinegar and vanilla extract.

2 Pile the meringue on to the prepared baking sheet and spread into a 23 cm (9 inch) round. Hollow out the centre slightly and bake in a preheated oven, 150°C (300°F), Gas Mark 2, for 1½ hours.

3 Leave to cool, then peel away the paper and place the pavlova on a serving plate.

4 To make the filling, whip the cream in a bowl until stiff and fold in some of the fruit and passion fruit pulp. Pile into the pavlova and decorate with the remaining fruit and passion fruit pulp.

Monte bianco

You have to pile this up and make it look like a snow-capped mountain, hence the name. I do like the creaminess and the soft, sweetened chestnuts.

1 Push the chestnuts through a sieve or a potato ricer and transfer to a bowl.

2 Put the rum, water, caster sugar and fennel seeds in a small, heavy-based saucepan and heat gently until the sugar has dissolved. Increase the heat and boil the liquid for about 5 minutes until reduced and syrupy. Strain the syrup into the chestnuts and beat well to mix, then taste and beat in more rum and sugar if you like.

3 Form the mixture into a single cone shape on a serving plate and chill in the refrigerator for 1–2 hours.

4 Whip the cream and icing sugar together in a bowl until the cream holds its shape. Swirl the cream all over the chestnut mound, as if you were icing a cake. Chill until ready to serve.

SERVES 6

3 x 250 g (8 oz) cans chestnuts, drained

50 ml (2 fl oz) rum, or to taste

125 ml (4 fl oz) water

50 g (2 oz) caster sugar, or to taste

2 tablespoons fennel seeds

250 ml (8 fl oz) double cream

2 tablespoons icing sugar, sifted

Old English trifle

I nearly fell out with John Torode when I insisted a contestant go through to a quarter final of *Masterchef* because of the quality of her trifle. It is a lovely dessert and it reminds me of my grandmother. This is a bit of a posh version: if you want to recreate my Nan's, use hundreds and thousands instead of crystallized petals on the top.

1 Slice the sponge cake in half horizontally, spread with the jam and sandwich it back together. If using sponge fingers, split them, spread the insides with the jam and sandwich back together. Cut the sponge into small pieces and place in the bottom of a serving bowl. Pour over the sherry and brandy.

2 Make the custard. Leave to cool slightly, then pour over the sponge cake and leave until cold.

3 Spread the whipped cream over the trifle and chill until ready to eat. Decorate with crystallized petals just before serving, if you like.

SERVES 8–10

23 cm (9 inch) sponge cake, or 6 sponge fingers (see page 182)

2–3 tablespoons seedless raspberry jam

4–5 tablespoons sherry

4–5 tablespoons brandy

1 quantity Proper Custard (see page 170) or double quantity Quick Custard (see page 170)

475 ml (16 fl oz) whipping cream, whipped

crystallized petals, to decorate (optional)

Crema catalana

SERVES 4

5 egg yolks

60 g (2¼ oz) caster sugar

2 tablespoons cornflour

600 ml (1 pint) full-fat milk

¼ teaspoon ground cinnamon

large pinch of freshly grated nutmeg

finely grated rind of 1 small lemon

60 g (2¼ oz) demerara or raw sugar

This gorgeous dessert is from Spain. It is similar to a crème brûlée but has the fragrance of vanilla with the zesty tang of lemon, and isn't quite as rich.

1 Beat the egg yolks, caster sugar and cornflour together in a bowl using a fork until smooth.

2 Pour the milk into a saucepan, add the cinnamon, nutmeg, and lemon rind and bring to the boil. Gradually stir the spiced milk into the egg yolk mixture, then return the milk mixture to the saucepan and bring to the boil, stirring constantly. Reduce the heat and cook for 2–3 minutes, still stirring, until the custard has thickened.

3 Divide the custard between 4 shallow 300 ml (½ pint) ceramic dishes and leave to cool. Chill for 3–4 hours.

4 About 20–30 minutes before serving, sprinkle the desserts with the demerara or raw sugar and caramelize with a blowtorch, then leave to stand at room temperature until ready to serve.

Gregg's tip

Grated orange rind can be used instead of the lemon rind, or a cinnamon stick instead of the ground cinnamon, but make sure you remove the cinnamon stick before pouring the custard into the serving dishes.

Tiramisù

SERVES 4

1 egg yolk

2 tablespoons caster sugar

1 teaspoon vanilla extract

250 g (8 oz) mascarpone cheese

125 ml (4 fl oz) strong black coffee

2 tablespoons brandy

1 tablespoon cocoa powder

16 amaretti biscuits (see page 186 for macaroons)

cocoa powder, to decorate

This translates as 'pick me up'. It must be the coffee in it. Though quite frankly when I eat a big bowl full all I want to do is lie down and have a snooze!

1 Beat the egg yolk and sugar together in a large bowl until smooth. Stir in the vanilla extract and mascarpone cheese until thoroughly combined, then set aside.

2 Mix the coffee, brandy and cocoa powder together in a separate bowl. Break up the amaretti biscuits and stir them into the coffee mixture, then divide half the mixture between 4 dessert bowls or glasses.

3 Spoon half the mascarpone mixture over the biscuit mixture. Add the remaining biscuit mixture and top with the remaining mascarpone mixture. Dust lightly with cocoa powder. Chill before serving.

Classic Grand Marnier soufflé

SERVES 4

butter, for greasing

100 g (3½ oz) caster sugar, plus 1 tablespoon for sprinkling

3 egg yolks

40 g (1½ oz) plain flour

250 ml (8 fl oz) milk

4 tablespoons Grand Marnier

finely grated rind of 2 oranges

5 egg whites

icing sugar, for dusting

Don't be scared of the soufflé! Especially one flavoured with Grand Marnier. You get a hint of booze and then it disappears because the soufflé is so light.

1 Thoroughly grease a 15 cm (6 inch) diameter x 9 cm (3¾ inch) deep soufflé dish making a lip of butter around the inside top rim, and sprinkle with the 1 tablespoon caster sugar to coat.

2 Whisk half the remaining caster sugar and egg yolks together in a bowl using a hand-held electric whisk until thick, pale and mousse-like. Sift the flour over the surface, then gently fold it in with a large metal spoon.

3 Bring the milk just to the boil in a saucepan, then gradually whisk it into the egg yolk mixture. Return the milk mixture to the pan and cook over a medium heat, stirring constantly, until thickened and smooth. Remove from the heat and stir in the Grand Marnier and orange rind. Cover and leave to cool.

4 Whisk the egg whites in a large, grease-free bowl into stiff, moist-looking peaks. Gradually whisk in the remaining caster sugar, a teaspoon at a time, until thick and glossy. Using a large metal spoon, fold a spoonful of egg whites into the cooled sauce to loosen, then gently fold in the remaining egg whites.

5 Spoon the mixture into the prepared dish and bake in a preheated oven, 220°C (425°F), Gas Mark 7, for 17–20 minutes until the soufflé is well risen, the top is browned and there is a slight wobble to the centre. Dust the soufflé with icing sugar and serve immediately.

ices and mousses

Old-fashioned vanilla ice cream

SERVES 6

300 ml (½ pint) single cream

1 vanilla pod, split lengthways

4 egg yolks

50 g (2 oz) caster sugar

300 ml (½ pint) double or whipping cream

A timeless classic. First the cold of the ice cream numbs the palate, then comes that lovely creamy texture and finally the heavenly taste of vanilla, the world's second most expensive spice.

1 Put the single cream and vanilla pod in a heavy-based saucepan and heat gently to just below boiling point. Remove from the heat and leave to infuse.

2 Meanwhile, put the egg yolks and caster sugar in a heatproof bowl set over a saucepan of simmering water so that the base of the bowl is not touching the water. Stir with a wooden spoon until thick and creamy, then gradually stir in the scalded single cream, removing the vanilla pod. Continue stirring for 15 minutes until the custard coats the back of the spoon. Remove the bowl from the pan and leave to cool.

3 Pour the vanilla mixture into an ice cream maker, add the double or whipping cream and churn and freeze, according to the manufacturer's instructions, until firm.

4 Alternatively, pour the vanilla mixture into a rigid, freezerproof container, cover and freeze for about 45 minutes or until slushy. Whip the double or whipping cream in a bowl until it just holds its shape. Remove the vanilla mixture from the freezer, beat thoroughly, then fold in the cream. Return the mixture to the container, cover and freeze for a further 45 minutes, then beat again until smooth. Freeze the ice cream for at least 1–2 hours.

5 Transfer the ice cream to the refrigerator for about 30 minutes to soften slightly before serving.

Gregg's tip

For an Italian-style treat make Affogato: simply pour freshly made espresso over the ice cream and serve immediately.

Rum and raisin ice

75 g (3 oz) seedless raisins

4 tablespoons dark rum

3 egg yolks

125 g (4 oz) soft light brown sugar

300 ml (½ pint) single cream

300 ml (½ pint) double cream, whipped

This is actually my favourite ice cream in the whole wide world. I first sampled it out shopping with my grandparents in Jones and Higgins department store in Peckham. I'm very proud to have had such a sophisticated palate at such a young age. I LOVE THIS ICE CREAM!

1 Soak the raisins in the rum in a bowl. Whisk the egg yolks and sugar together in a heatproof bowl using a hand-held electric whisk until thick, pale and mousse-like.

2 Put the single cream in a heavy-based saucepan and heat gently to just below boiling point. Stir into the egg mixture. Place the bowl over a saucepan of simmering water so that the base of the bowl is not touching the water and stir until thickened. Strain and leave to cool.

3 Fold the double cream into the cooled custard mixture. Transfer to a rigid, freezerproof container, cover and freeze for 2–3 hours until there is 2.5 cm (1 inch) solid ice cream around the sides. Beat until smooth, then stir in the rum and raisins. Return to the freezer and freeze until firm.

4 Transfer the ice cream to the refrigerator for about 20 minutes to soften slightly before serving. Scoop into chilled glasses to serve.

Coffee hazelnut ice

This ice cream is simply amazing. A slow build up of flavours as the ice cream melts in your mouth – bitter coffee, toasted nuts, sugar and cream. Very grown up.

1 Reserve a few hazelnuts for decoration, then grind the remainder coarsely. Put the milk in a heavy-based saucepan and heat gently to just below boiling point. Whisk the egg yolks and sugar together in a bowl using a hand-held electric whisk until thick, pale and mousse-like. Gradually whisk in the hot milk, then stir in the ground nuts.

2 Pour the mixture into a clean saucepan and heat gently, stirring constantly, until the mixture is thick enough to coat the back of the spoon. Do not allow it to boil. Stir in the coffee, mixing well to blend. Cover and leave until cold, stirring occasionally.

3 Fold the whipped cream into the coffee custard. Turn into individual rigid, freezerproof containers, cover and freeze until firm. Transfer to the refrigerator about 1 hour to soften before serving. Decorate with the reserved nuts and mint sprigs and serve with dessert biscuits.

SERVES 4–5

100 g (3½ oz) hazelnuts, toasted and skinned

300 ml (½ pint) milk

4 egg yolks

75 g (3 oz) caster sugar

1 tablespoon instant coffee granules

175 ml (6 fl oz) whipping cream, whipped

mint sprigs, to decorate

dessert biscuits, to serve

Spiced mango sorbet with pineapple

SERVES 8

1 pineapple, cut into 8 wedges, cored and skin removed

175 g (6 oz) palm sugar

3 mangoes, peeled and stoned

3 teaspoons finely grated fresh root ginger

1 fresh or frozen kaffir lime leaf, stem removed

½ red chilli, deseeded

100 ml (3½ fl oz) freshly squeezed lime juice

50 ml (2 fl oz) clear honey

Very clever this. The ginger and the chilli act as a slight irritant for your taste buds, teasing them until the honeyed warm juice of the pineapple comes flooding in and sweeps you away to a tropical island.

1 Place the pineapple wedges on a foil-lined metal tray and sprinkle with half the palm sugar. Cover with clingfilm and leave to marinate for at least an hour.

2 Put all the remaining ingredients, except the remaining palm sugar, into a blender and blend for 2 minutes, then add the palm sugar and blend for a further 10–15 seconds.

3 Transfer the purée to an ice cream maker and churn and freeze, according to the manufacturer's instructions, until firm – about 30–45 minutes. Transfer to a dish, cover and put in the freezer.

4 Lay the marinated pineapple on a foil-lined tray and cook under a preheated very hot grill on all sides until it begins to caramelize. Transfer to a plate and leave to cool. Reserve any juices that may have come out in the marinade and pour over the pineapple.

5 To serve, place a scoop of the sorbet onto each plate and add a pineapple wedge.

Champagne sorbet

SERVES 8

300 g (10 oz) caster sugar

250 ml (8 fl oz) water

600 ml (1 pint) sparkling white wine

3 tablespoons freshly squeezed lemon juice

2 egg whites

4 tablespoons icing sugar

Oh so very posh! People will be really impressed with this. It contrasts between sharp and sweet with an undercurrent of boozy sophistication.

1 Put the caster sugar and water in a saucepan and heat gently until the sugar has dissolved. Bring to the boil and boil for about 5 minutes or until thick but not beginning to brown. Remove from the heat and leave to cool, then stir in 350 ml (12 fl oz) of the wine and the lemon juice. Pour into freezer trays and freeze for about 1 hour or until mushy.

2 Pour the mixture into a bowl and beat well for 2 minutes. Return to the freezer trays and freeze for a further 30 minutes. Beat again. Repeat the freezing and beating every 30 minutes for the next 2 hours.

3 Beat the egg whites in a grease-free bowl until stiff. Gradually beat in the icing sugar.

4 Beat the frozen mixture well to break down the ice crystals, then fold in the egg white mixture. Return to the freezer and freeze until the sorbet is firm.

5 Transfer the sorbet to the refrigerator for about 30 minutes to soften slightly before serving. Pour a little of the remaining wine over each portion.

Earl Grey sorbet

Sorbets are great, you get a hit of sweetness but because they are ice they are so cleansing as well. The subtle flavoured Earl Grey gives a lovely aftertaste.

1 Put the tea in a heatproof bowl and pour over the boiling water. Add the lemon rind and juice and sugar. Leave until cold, then strain into a rigid, freezerproof container. Cover and freeze for about 2 hours until mushy.

2 Whisk the egg whites in a grease-free bowl until stiff, then beat into the frozen mixture. Return to the freezer for 2 hours, then beat again and freeze until firm.

3 Transfer the sorbet to the refrigerator for 30–50 minutes to soften before serving. Scoop into chilled glasses to serve.

SERVES 4

4 teaspoons Earl Grey tea

450 ml (¾ pint) boiling water

finely pared rind and juice of 1 lemon

75 g (3 oz) caster sugar

2 egg whites

Lemon granita

SERVES 4

125 g (4 oz) caster sugar

600 ml (1 pint) water

thinly pared rind and juice of 3 lemons

Classic Italian, something I'm always keen on. The lemon flavour is so fresh, so clean it takes you to the edge of sharpness then quickly turns to sweetness. Sharp and sweet together with ice, it's like an Alpine shower!

1 Put the sugar, water and lemon rind in a saucepan and heat gently until the sugar has dissolved. Bring to the boil and boil for 5 minutes. Stir in the lemon juice and leave to cool, then strain.

2 Pour into a rigid, freezerproof container, cover and freeze for 2 hours. Whisk and return to the freezer for 2 hours. Whisk again and return to the freezer until firm.

3 To serve, leave at room temperature for 10 minutes, then stir until crumbly. Spoon into tall glasses and serve immediately.

Mocha semi-freddo

SERVES 5–6

250 g (8 oz) mascarpone cheese

2 tablespoons brandy

2 tablespoons finely ground espresso coffee

25 g (1 oz) icing sugar

75 g (3 oz) bitter or plain chocolate, grated

5 tablespoons single cream

300 ml (½ pint) double cream

TO DECORATE

coffee-flavoured liqueur (optional)

lightly whipped cream

This dessert actually brings together a wonderful selection of some of my favourite ingredients. And it's easy to make too – you just need to allow time for it to freeze.

1 Beat the mascarpone, brandy, espresso coffee and icing sugar together in a bowl. Reserve 1 tablespoon of the grated chocolate, then stir the remainder and the single cream into the mixture.

2 Whip the double cream in a bowl until just peaking. Using a large metal spoon, fold the cream into the mascarpone mixture.

3 Turn the chocolate mixture into a rigid, freezerproof container and freeze for 2–3 hours.

4 To serve, scoop the semi-freddo into serving glasses or coffee cups. Drizzle with a little coffee-flavoured liqueur, if you like. Decorate with lightly whipped cream and serve sprinkled with the reserved grated chocolate.

Zabaglione

This is remarkably easy to make but it leaves a powerful impression. It has a texture like no other, sticky but not heavy. The taste has real depth from the Marsala. It's a classic Italian dessert, one that is appearing on more and more restaurant menus.

1 Whisk the egg yolks and sugar together in a heatproof bowl using a hand-held electric whisk until pale and foamy.

2 Set the bowl over a saucepan of almost boiling water so that the base of the bowl is not touching the water. Whisk in the Marsala. Continue whisking until the mixture expands to form a dense, foamy mass that just holds its shape.

3 Spoon the zabaglione into wine glasses and serve immediately with sponge fingers.

SERVES 4

4 egg yolks

50 g (2 oz) caster sugar

8 tablespoons Marsala

sponge fingers, to serve
(see page 182)

Passion fruit and lime soufflé mousse

Passion fruit and lime, sweetened with sugar, is a heady concoction, I promise you. This is a fab mousse and worth making if only to fill your kitchen with this heavenly scent.

1 Using kitchen string, tie a double thickness band of baking paper around the top of a 13 cm (5½ inch) diameter x 6 cm (2½ inch) deep soufflé dish so that it stands 6 cm (2½ inches) higher than the top of the dish. Alternatively, use 6 large espresso or medium tea cups.

2 Put the water in a small heatproof bowl or mug and sprinkle over the gelatine, making sure that the water absorbs all the powder. Set aside for 5 minutes, then stand the bowl in a small saucepan half-filled with boiling water and simmer for 3–4 minutes, stirring occasionally, until the gelatine dissolves to a clear liquid.

3 Put the egg yolks, sugar and lime rind in a large, heatproof bowl set over a saucepan of simmering water so that the base of the bowl is not touching the water. Whisk using a hand-held electric whisk for about 10 minutes until the mixture is very thick, and the whisk leaves a trail when lifted. Gradually whisk in the lime juice and whisk until thick again. Remove the bowl from the pan and continue whisking until cool.

4 Gradually fold in the dissolved gelatine, adding it in a thin, steady stream. Scoop the seeds out of 6 of the passion fruit and fold into the soufflé mixture.

5 Softly whip the cream in a bowl (no need to wash the whisk in between), then fold into the soufflé mixture. Chill for 20–30 minutes until just beginning to set. Lightly stir the mixture to redistribute any passion fruit seeds that may have sunk to the bottom.

6 Whisk the egg whites in a large, grease-free bowl into stiff, moist peaks. Using a large metal spoon, fold a large spoonful of egg whites into the soufflé mixture to loosen, then gently fold in the remaining egg whites. Pour the mixture into the prepared soufflé dish so that it stands above the rim of the dish. Chill for 4 hours or until set. To serve, gently remove the soufflé collar and top the soufflé with seeds scooped from the remaining 2 passion fruit.

SERVES 6

4 tablespoons water

4 teaspoons powdered gelatine

4 eggs, separated

175 g (6 oz) caster sugar

finely grated rind of 3 limes

5 tablespoons freshly squeezed lime juice

8 passion fruit, halved

250 ml (8 fl oz) double cream

White chocolate and pistachio mousse

SERVES 6

75 g (3 oz) shelled pistachio nuts

200 g (7 oz) white chocolate, chopped

150 ml (¼ pint) double cream

1 teaspoon vanilla paste or ½ teaspoon vanilla extract

150 ml (¼ pint) natural yogurt

4 egg whites

icing sugar, for dusting

Ok sugar fiends this one is for you. It's rich, it's sweet and at least with each spoonful you'll know why you are putting inches on your hips.

1 Put the nuts in a heatproof bowl, cover with boiling water and leave for 1 minute. Drain well and rub between several layers of kitchen paper to remove the skins. Transfer the nuts to a food processor, finely chop and set aside.

2 Put the chocolate with 3 tablespoons of the cream in a large, heatproof bowl set over a saucepan of barely simmering water so that the base of the bowl is not touching the water and leave until melted, stirring gently once or twice until smooth.

3 Lightly whip the remaining cream and vanilla paste together in a bowl until very lightly peaking. Stir in the yogurt. Beat the egg whites in a large, grease-free bowl until just peaking.

4 Beat the cream mixture into the melted chocolate, then fold in the egg whites using a large metal spoon. Spoon half the mousse into 6 small glass dishes or cups. Reserve some of the nuts for decoration and sprinkle the rest over the mousse. Add the remaining mousse and decorate with the reserved nuts. Chill for at least 1 hour until lightly set and serve dusted with icing sugar.

Strawberry mousse

There aren't that many ingredients to a mousse but you do have to make it quite carefully. Take your time and concentrate and it will all come good I promise. It's a lovely skill to have mastered, a mousse, and this one is divine.

1 Purée the strawberries in an electric blender, then sieve to remove any pips; there should be 250 ml (8 fl oz) purée.

2 Place the eggs, egg yolk and sugar in a heatproof bowl set over a saucepan of barely simmering water so that the base of the bowl is not touching the water. Whisk until thick.

3 Place the orange juice in a small pan, sprinkle over the gelatine and leave for 5 minutes. Heat gently to dissolve the gelatine, then fold into the egg mousse with the strawberry purée and the cream.

4 Stir the mousse mixture over a bowl of iced water until it begins to set, then turn into one 900 ml (1½ pint) dish or mould, or 6 x 150 ml (¼ pint) ramekins or moulds. Chill until set. If using moulds, turn the mousses out onto a serving plate (or plates). Serve with a few strawberries dusted with icing sugar, if you like.

SERVES 6

350 g (12 oz) fresh strawberries

2 eggs

1 egg yolk

75 g (3 oz) caster sugar

3 tablespoons orange juice

15 g (½ oz) gelatine

150 ml (5 fl oz) double cream, lightly whipped

fresh strawberries dusted with icing sugar, to decorate (optional)

**basics
and bites**

Vanilla sugar

MAKES 200 G (7 OZ)

2 vanilla pods

200 g (7 oz) caster sugar

Vanilla, although fantastic, is very expensive. This is a wonderful way of getting every ounce of vanilla flavour from your pod.

1 Use a small, sharp knife to cut each vanilla pod in half lengthways, then cut each length in half to make 8 pieces.

2 Put the sugar in a glass jar and push the vanilla pieces into it. Cover with the lid and store for about a week before using, shaking the jar occasionally to disperse the vanilla flavour.

Sugar syrup

MAKES 125 ML (4 FL OZ), enough to soak one 23 cm (9 inch) sandwich cake

125 g (4 oz) granulated sugar

150 ml (¼ pint) water

liqueur or spirit of your choice, for flavouring (optional)

A very practical way of adding sweetness, it helps keep your puddings moist and because it's a syrup it doesn't crystallize. Everything is soft and moist without having a brittle crunch.

1 Put the sugar and water in a saucepan and heat gently until dissolved. Bring to a rolling boil and boil for 1 minute.

2 Remove from the heat and leave to cool. If you like, flavour with any liqueur or spirit to whatever strength you desire.

Apricot glaze

This does give a wonderful glossy finish to pastry. Its sweet but slightly tart taste gives it a great point of difference. It even works brushed on to fresh fruit.

1 Put the jam and water in a small saucepan and heat gently until the jam has melted. Add the lemon juice.

2 Strain the mixture and return to the pan, then simmer until syrupy. Use warm.

MAKES 125 G (4 OZ)

125 g (4 oz) apricot jam

2 tablespoons water

squeeze of lemon juice

Glacé icing

Anybody with a keen eye for decoration needs to know how to make this icing. It is very simple and armed with some food colourings the possibilities are endless.

1 Sift the icing sugar into a bowl and gradually add the water. The icing should be thick enough to coat the back of the spoon thickly.

2 Add flavouring or food colouring, if required, and use immediately.

Flavourings

Chocolate: Sift 3 tablespoons cocoa powder with the icing sugar.

Coffee: Replace 1 tablespoon warm water with 1 tablespoon coffee essence.

Orange or Lemon: Replace 1 tablespoon warm water with 1 tablespoon freshly squeezed orange or lemon juice. Add the finely grated rind of 1 orange or lemon and a few drops of orange or yellow food colouring.

MAKES ENOUGH TO ICE 18–24 SMALL CAKES; half the quantity will ice the top of a 20 cm (8 inch) round cake

250 g (8 oz) icing sugar

about 2 tablespoons warm water

flavouring (see below) or a few drops of food colouring (optional)

Quick custard

SERVES 2–4

2 egg yolks

1 teaspoon cornflour

2 tablespoons caster sugar

300 ml (½ pint) milk

½ teaspoon vanilla extract

This is a very clever cheat's custard. It's not as rich and deep as the real stuff but it's not a bad quick alternative. Not bad at all.

1 Beat the egg yolks, cornflour and sugar together in a bowl until pale and creamy.

2 Bring the milk to the boil in a saucepan, pour on to the egg mixture and stir. Return the mixture to the cleaned saucepan and cook over a gentle heat, stirring constantly with a wooden spoon, until the mixture is thick enough to coat the back of the spoon.

3 Add the vanilla extract, then strain. Serve warm.

Proper custard

SERVES 6

1 vanilla pod

3 bay leaves or 3 rosemary sprigs (optional)

325 ml (11 fl oz) milk

325 ml (11 fl oz) single cream

6 egg yolks

2 tablespoons caster sugar

The French with all their culinary expertise know a good thing when they see it and have at least credited the English with possibly the best pudding invention ever: big rich egg custard, nothing quite like it. Everybody should learn how to make it.

1 Use the tip of a small, sharp knife to score the vanilla pod lengthways through to the centre. Put it in a heavy-based saucepan with the bay leaves or rosemary sprigs, if using, milk and cream and bring the mixture slowly to the boil. Remove from the heat and leave to infuse for 20 minutes.

2 Beat the egg yolks and sugar together in a bowl. Remove the herb and vanilla pod from the milk, scrape out the seeds of the vanilla pod with the tip of a knife and return them to the milk.

3 Pour the milk over the egg mixture, beating well. Return the mixture to the cleaned saucepan and cook over a very gentle heat, stirring constantly with a wooden spoon, until the sauce is thick enough to coat the back of the spoon. This may take up to 10 minutes. Serve warm.

Quick crème pâtissière

MAKES ABOUT 300 ML
(½ PINT)

1 egg, plus 1 egg yolk

50 g (2 oz) caster sugar

40 g (1½ oz) plain flour

300 ml (½ pint) milk

¼ teaspoon vanilla extract
or almond essence, or to
taste

**This is a good one to play with because it has a lot of flour.
You still get the lovely flavour but it's quick to make and
easy to handle.**

1 Beat the eggs and sugar together in a bowl until smooth and
nearly white. Gradually stir in the flour and then the milk. Pour
into a small saucepan and bring to the boil, stirring constantly.
Reduce the heat and simmer for 3–5 minutes, stirring, to cook the
flour thoroughly.

2 If a thick cream is required, cook for a few minutes longer to
reduce the liquid.

3 Flavour to taste with vanilla extract or almond essence, then
turn into a bowl and leave to cool, stirring occasionally to prevent
a skin from forming.

Rich crème pâtissière

MAKES ABOUT 300 ML
(½ PINT)

150 ml (¼ pint) milk

150 ml (¼ pint) double
cream

1 vanilla pod

4 egg yolks

3 tablespoons caster sugar

2 tablespoons plain flour

**Don't be scared: if you can make custard you can make
this. It really is just like custard with flour added to
stabilize it, which means it's a bit firmer. So you can fill
tarts with it.**

1 Put the milk and cream in a heavy-based saucepan. Use the tip of
a small, sharp knife to score the vanilla pod lengthways through to
the centre. Add it to the pan and bring the mixture to the boil.
Remove from the heat and leave to infuse for 20 minutes.

2 Beat the egg yolks, sugar and flour together in a bowl until smooth.
Remove the vanilla pod from the milk, scrape out the seeds with the
tip of a knife and return them to the milk. Pour the milk over the egg
mixture, beating well.

3 Return the custard to the pan and cook over a gentle heat, stirring
constantly with a wooden spoon, for 4–5 minutes until thick and
smooth. Turn the custard into a small bowl and leave to cool, covered
with greaseproof paper to prevent a skin from forming.

Butter cream

This is an egg free icing essential for decorating little cup cakes as well as many other pastries and cakes. The butter gives it richness and creaminess.

1 Beat the butter with half the icing sugar in a bowl until smooth.

2 Add the remaining icing sugar with the milk, flavouring and food colouring, if using. Beat until creamy.

Flavourings

Chocolate: Blend 2 tablespoons cocoa powder with 2 tablespoons boiling water. Leave to cool, then add to the mixture with only 1 tablespoon milk.

Coffee: Replace 1 tablespoon milk with 1 tablespoon coffee essence.

Mocha: Blend 1 teaspoon cocoa powder and 2 teaspoons instant coffee powder with 1 tablespoon boiling water. Leave to cool, then add to the mixture with only 1 tablespoon milk.

Orange or Lemon: Add the finely grated rind of 1 orange or lemon. Replace the milk with freshly squeezed orange or lemon juice. Add a few drops of orange or yellow food colouring, if you like.

MAKES ENOUGH TO FILL AND COVER A 20 CM (8 INCH) SANDWICH CAKE

125 g (4 oz) unsalted butter, softened

300 g (10 oz) icing sugar, sifted

2 tablespoons milk

flavouring (see left) or food colouring (optional)

Brandy butter

I don't mind admitting that this is one of my favourite flavours in the whole world. I know you shouldn't have favourites, but I do. This with cream on top of a Christmas pudding is my idea of heaven.

1 Beat the butter in a bowl until soft. Gradually add the sugar and brandy, beating thoroughly with each addition.

2 Pile into a serving dish. Cover and chill until firm.

SERVES 6

150 g (5 oz) unsalted butter

150 g (5 oz) caster sugar

3–4 tablespoons brandy

Chocolate ganache

MAKES ABOUT 350 ML
(12 FL OZ)

175 ml (6 fl oz) double
cream

175 g (6 oz) plain
chocolate, broken into
pieces

This is a proper grown-up chocolate sauce. Once you've mastered it you can then play around with the consistency. It could be used warm and unwhisked to pour like a sauce, or cooler and firmer as a filling for a big chocolate cake.

1 Bring the cream just to the boil in a small saucepan. Remove from the heat and add the chocolate.

2 Stir gently until the chocolate has melted. Transfer to a bowl.

3 Leave the mixture to cool slightly, then whisk until thickened to the desired consistency.

Variation

Add a dash of brandy, rum or orange-flavoured liqueur with the chocolate.

Chocolate sauce

MAKES 450 ML (3/4 PINT)

175 g (6 oz) plain
chocolate, chopped

250 ml (8 fl oz) milk

1 teaspoon instant coffee
granules

50 g (2 oz) soft light brown
sugar

Come on, everybody needs to be able to make a chocolate sauce. Sticky, creamy, heady cocoa flavour. It goes with just about everything.

1 Put all the ingredients in a small saucepan and heat very gently until melted.

2 Stir well, reduce the heat and simmer, uncovered, for 2–3 minutes.

Shortcrust pastry

MAKES 200 G (7 OZ)

200 g (7 oz) plain flour, plus extra for dusting

pinch of salt

100 g (3½ oz) butter or equal quantities of butter and white vegetable fat

2–3 tablespoons iced water

This is the pastry you want for a tart or a pie. It doesn't rise or fluff up when you bake it and has a crunch that melts in the mouth.

1 Sift the flour and salt into a bowl. Cut the butter, and fat if using, into small pieces and add it to the flour.

2 Rub the butter, and fat if using, into the flour with your fingertips very lightly and evenly until the mixture resembles fine breadcrumbs. Add just enough of the water, stirring it in with a palette knife, for the mixture to begin to bind together into a dough.

3 Turn the dough out on a lightly floured surface and knead briefly. Wrap in foil and chill for 30 minutes before using.

Cheat's rough puff pastry

MAKES 250 G (8 OZ)

250 g (8 oz) plain flour, plus extra for dusting

pinch of salt

175 g (6 oz butter), thoroughly chilled

2 teaspoons freshly squeezed lemon juice

about 150 ml (¼ pint) iced water

Yes, you can buy ready-rolled but have a go at this foolproof way of delivering this most versatile of pastries, perfectly every time.

1 Sift the flour and salt into a bowl. Holding the butter with cool fingertips, or by its folded-back wrapper, grate it coarsely into the flour. Work quickly before the butter softens from the heat of your hand.

2 Stir the grated butter into the flour with a palette knife. Add the lemon juice and enough of the water, stirring it in with the palette knife, for the mixture to begin to bind together into a dough.

3 Turn out the dough on a lightly floured surface and knead briefly until smooth. Roll it out into an oblong about 3 times longer than it is wide.

4 Fold the bottom third of the pastry up and the top third down, then press around the sides with a rolling pin to seal the layers together lightly. Wrap in foil and chill for 30 minutes before using.

Pâté sucrée

Exactly the same as shortcrust pastry but with sugar in it, so it's perfect for sweet pies and tarts.

1 Sift the flour and salt into a pile on to a cold surface and make a well in the centre.

2 Add the butter, egg yolks, water and sugar to the well and use the fingertips of one hand to work them together into a rough paste. The mixture should resemble scrambled egg.

3 Gradually work in the flour with your fingertips to bind the mixture into a smooth dough. Press together lightly and form into a ball. Wrap in foil and chill for 30 minutes before using.

MAKES 175 G (6 OZ), enough to line a 20 cm (8 inch) flan tin

175 g (6 oz) plain flour

pinch of salt

75 g (3 oz) unsalted butter, slightly softened

2 egg yolks

1 tablespoon iced water

40 g (1½ oz) caster sugar

Choux pastry

Yummy! I love this pastry. It's light – almost weightless – and used to make profiteroles and éclairs. You know you want to make this, you know you do. Please, it's my favourite pastry.

1 Sift the flour on to a sheet of greaseproof paper.

2 Put the water, butter and salt in a saucepan and bring to the boil over a medium heat. Remove from the heat, add the flour all at once and beat hard with a wooden spoon for about 20 seconds until the mixture comes away from the side of the pan. Return the pan to a very low heat and beat the mixture for about 30 seconds.

3 Leave the mixture to cool slightly. Beat in the eggs a little at a time, beating hard after each addition, using just enough egg to make a glossy dough that falls from the spoon. Use the pastry immediately or cover closely and chill until needed.

MAKES ENOUGH FOR 8–10 LARGE PROFITEROLES OR 20 SMALL PROFITEROLES

65 g (2½ oz) plain flour

150 ml (¼ pint) water

50 g (2 oz butter), diced, plus extra for greasing

pinch of salt

2 large eggs, beaten

Hot caramel sauce

MAKES 300 ML (½ PINT)

200 ml (7 fl oz) water

75 g (3 oz) caster sugar

juice of ½ lemon

Oh my word! Another absolutely out of this world flavour experience. Slightly bitter start but a nice warm sugary finish. There is somebody up there looking after our wellbeing. How else can you explain the wonder of caramel sauce?

1 Pour 150 ml (¼ pint) of the water into a heavy-based saucepan and add the sugar. Heat gently until the sugar has dissolved.

2 Increase the heat and cook rapidly until the syrup begins to caramelize. The temperature should register 177°C (350°F) on a sugar thermometer – the caramel stage.

3 Remove from the heat and gradually stir in the remaining water with the lemon juice. Leave to cool, then gently reheat the sauce before serving.

Butterscotch sauce

MAKES 250 ML (8 FL OZ)

150 ml (¼ pint) double cream

50 g (2 oz) unsalted butter

75 g (3 oz) soft dark brown sugar

Yet another flavour I simply can't live without. I first encountered it as a child in Angel Delight, would you believe, and once sampled I was completely hooked.

1 Put the cream, butter and sugar in a saucepan and heat gently, stirring, until the sugar has dissolved.

2 Bring the mixture to the boil and boil for 2 minutes until syrupy.

Hot fudge sauce

Sweetness of course but buttery, cocoa flavour with just a hint of salt. Just a hint mind. I can't think of anything better poured over ice cream.

SERVES 6

75 g (3 oz) unsalted butter, diced

140 g (4½ oz) soft light brown sugar

175 g (6 oz) can evaporated milk

2 teaspoons vanilla extract

1 Put the butter and sugar in a small, heavy-based saucepan and heat very gently, stirring with a wooden spoon, until the butter has melted and the sugar has dissolved.

2 Bring the mixture to the boil and boil for about 2 minutes or until the syrup has the consistency of treacle. Remove from the heat.

3 Stir in the evaporated milk and vanilla extract and return the mixture to the heat. Bring to the boil and boil for about a minute until the sauce is smooth and glossy. Serve warm.

Gregg's tip

Stir 1 tablespoon Tia Maria into the finished sauce.

Raspberry coulis

A very good blend of sharpness and sweetness, raspberry has its own very defined taste. It adds an ever so slight bitterness that helps to enhance other flavours on the plate.

SERVES 4

300 g (10 oz) raspberries, defrosted if frozen

2 tablespoons caster sugar

1 Purée the raspberries in a blender or food processor.

2 Press the puréed raspberries through a nylon sieve into a bowl, then stir in the sugar.

Brandy snaps

My grandmother used to make these for me. She used to serve them with clotted cream, and I used to let some of them go soggy before eating them. Truly delicious.

1 Put the butter, sugar and syrup in a saucepan and heat gently until the butter has melted and the sugar has dissolved. Leave to cool slightly, then sift in the flour and ginger. Beat well.

2 Place teaspoonfuls of the mixture 10 cm (4 inches) apart on baking sheets. Bake in a preheated oven, 180°C (350°F), Gas Mark 4, for 10–12 minutes until golden.

3 Leave to cool slightly, then remove with a palette knife and roll around the handle of a wooden spoon. Leave for 1–2 minutes to set, then slip off carefully on to a wire rack to cool completely.

MAKES 35

125 g (4 oz) butter

125 g (4 oz) demerara sugar

125 g (4 oz) golden syrup

125 g (4 oz) plain flour

1 teaspoon ground ginger

Tuile biscuits

Oh, we are getting sophisticated now. This is professional stuff. The name actually derives from the French word for tile. Its curved shape is supposed to represent the curved roofing tile you see around the Mediterranean.

1 Grease a baking sheet. Sift the icing sugar and flour into a bowl. Add the egg white, then the melted butter and stir to blend together until smooth.

2 Drop 6 large spoonfuls of the mixture on to the prepared baking sheet and spread out slightly to form 6 biscuits, leaving at least 3.5 cm (1½ inches) between them to allow for spreading. Bake in a preheated oven, 180°C (350°F), Gas Mark 4, for about 10 minutes until golden.

3 Working quickly, take the biscuits from the baking sheet and curl over a rolling pin while still warm and soft. If you want to make the tuile shape, now is the time to do it! Leave to cool completely.

MAKES 6

50 g (2 oz) icing sugar

50 g (2 oz) plain flour

50 ml (2 fl oz) egg white (about 1 extra-large egg)

40 g (1½ oz) butter, melted, plus extra for greasing

Sponge fingers

Light and fluffy with a slight crunch to the topping. Really good dunked in coffee, tea or dessert wine.

MAKES 22

butter, for greasing

50 g (2 oz) caster sugar, plus extra for dusting

2 eggs

a few drops of vanilla extract

50 g (2 oz) plain flour, sifted, plus extra for dusting

1 Grease and flour 2 baking sheets. Whisk the sugar, eggs and vanilla extract together in a bowl using a hand-held electric whisk until thick enough to leave a trail when the whisk is lifted. Fold in the flour with a large metal spoon.

2 Transfer the mixture to a piping bag fitted with a 1 cm (½ inch) plain nozzle and pipe into finger lengths on to the prepared baking sheets. Dust well with caster sugar and bake in a preheated oven, 190°C (375°F), Gas Mark 5, for 6–8 minutes until golden brown. Transfer to a wire rack to cool.

Vanilla biscotti

Fantastic, classic Italian biscuit. What you want to do is dip them in pudding wine. Vin Santo is the Italians' dip of choice.

MAKES 24

75 g (3 oz) whole unblanched almonds

50 g (2 oz) unsalted butter, softened, plus extra for greasing

100 g (3½ oz) caster sugar

140 g (4½ oz) self-raising flour, plus extra for dusting

1½ teaspoons baking powder

1 teaspoon ground coriander

65 g (2½ oz) ground almonds

2 eggs

finely grated rind of 1 lemon

2 teaspoons vanilla extract

icing sugar, for dusting

1 Grease a large baking sheet. Spread the almonds out on a separate dry baking sheet and lightly toast under a preheated medium grill for 1–2 minutes. Leave the almonds to cool, then chop coarsely.

2 Beat the butter and caster sugar together in a bowl until pale and fluffy. Sift the flour, baking powder and coriander into the bowl. Stir in the ground and toasted chopped almonds. Beat the eggs, lemon rind and vanilla extract together and add the mixture to the bowl. Mix to a soft dough. Turn the dough out on to a lightly floured surface and cut it in half. Shape each piece into a log about 23 cm (9 inches) long. Transfer the 2 pieces to the prepared baking sheet, spacing them well apart, and flatten each one to about 1 cm (½ inch) thick.

3 Bake the logs in a preheated oven, 160°C (325°F), Gas Mark 3, for about 30 minutes until they are risen and just firm. Leave to cool, then cut each log across into about 12 thin slices. Return the slices to the oven and bake for a further 10 minutes until crisp. Transfer the biscotti to a wire rack to cool and serve dusted with icing sugar.

Meringues

I pride myself on the quality of my meringues (ooh-er missus!). Brittle on the outside and slightly chewy in the middle. These are screaming out for some fruit and whipped cream.

MAKES 250 G (8 OZ) MERINGUE

4 egg whites

250 g (8 oz) caster sugar

1 teaspoon freshly squeezed lemon juice

1 Line 2 baking sheets with silicone paper. Whisk the egg whites in a large, grease-free bowl until very stiff and dry – if the meringue slides around the bowl when tilted, carry on whisking.

2 Add the sugar a tablespoon at a time, whisking very thoroughly after each addition. Finally, whisk in the lemon juice. The meringue should be smooth, glossy and form soft peaks.

3 Spoon into mounds or pipe into two 20–23 cm (8–9 inch) rounds on to the prepared baking sheets. Bake in a preheated oven, 140°C (275°F), Gas Mark 1, for 1½–2 hours until crisp. Peel away the paper and leave to cool on a wire rack. Use as required.

Macaroons

We are now entering the world of petit fours. Beautiful little delicate things macaroons. Can you imagine how superior you would feel serving tea with your own homemade macaroons?

MAKES 25

250 g (8 oz) caster sugar

150 g (5 oz) ground almonds

1 tablespoon rice flour

2 egg whites

1 sheet of rice paper

25 blanched almonds, split

1 Line a baking sheet with rice paper. Mix the sugar, ground almonds and rice flour together in a bowl.

2 In a separate bowl, beat the egg whites lightly, then add the dry ingredients and beat to a smooth, firm consistency.

3 Leave to stand for 5 minutes, then roll into small balls and place, slightly apart, on the prepared baking sheet. Flatten slightly and place a split almond on each one.

4 Bake the macaroons in a preheated oven, 180°C (350°F), Gas Mark 4, for 20 minutes. Leave to cool on the baking sheet. Cut off the rice paper around each macaroon and serve.

index

Acknowledgements

Executive Editor **Katy Denny**
Senior Editor **Charlotte Macey**
Creative Director **Tracy Killick**
Designer **Miranda Harvey**
Senior Production Controller **Amanda Mackie**
Photographer **Jason Lowe**
Food Stylist **Claire Ptak**
Special Photography: **© Octopus Publishing Group Limited/Jason Lowe**